Adventure into the New Age

*Cycle C Sermons for
Pentecost Through Proper 12
Based on the Gospel Texts*

Maurice A. Fetty

CSS Publishing Company, Inc.
Lima, Ohio

ADVENTURING INTO THE NEW AGE

FIRST EDITION
Copyright © 2012
by CSS Publishing Co., Inc.

Published by CSS Publishing Company, Inc., Lima, Ohio 45807. All rights reserved. No part of this publication may be reproduced in any manner whatsoever without the prior permission of the publisher, except in the case of brief quotations embodied in critical articles and reviews. Inquiries should be addressed to: CSS Publishing Company, Inc., Permissions Department, 5450 N. Dixie Highway, Lima, Ohio 45807.

Scripture quotations are from the Revised Standard Version of the Bible, copyrighted 1946, 1952 ©, 1971, 1973, by the Division of Christian Education of the National Council of the Churches of Christ in the USA. Used by permission.

Some quotations are marked NEB from The New English Bible. Copyright © the Delegates of the Oxford University Press and the Syndics of the Cambridge University Press, 1961, 1970. Reprinted by permission.

Library of Congress Cataloging-in-Publication Data
Fetty, Maurice A., 1936-
   Adventuring into the New Age : cycle C sermons for Pentecost 1, Pentecost Day through Proper 12, based on the Gospel texts / Maurice A. Fetty. -- 1st ed.
     p. cm.
   ISBN 0-7880-2679-8 (alk. paper)
   1. Bible. N.T. Luke--sermons. 2. Pentecost season--Sermons. 3. Common lectionary (1992) I. Title.

BS2595.54.F48 2012
252'.64--dc23

2012004190

For more information about CSS Publishing Company resources, visit our website at www.csspub.com, email us at csr@csspub.com, or call (800) 241-4056.

ISBN-13: 978-0-7880-2679-9
ISBN-10: 0-7880-2679-8   PRINTED IN USA

To the churches I have served over the years:

*Fairfax Christian Church, Indianapolis, Indiana
South Side Christian Church, Kokomo, Indiana
Flatbush Christian Church, Brooklyn, New York
La Hermosa Christian Church, East Harlem, New York
Colonial (Congregational) Church, Edina (Minneapolis), Minnesota
Mayflower Congregational Church, Grand Rapids, Michigan
The Congregational Church of Manhasset (UCC), Manhasset, New York
Park Congregational Church (UCC), Grand Rapids, Michigan*

Introduction

The prophecies of Advent, the lullabies of Christmas and the fanfares of Easter have ended. After fifty days, the season of Pentecost has come. It is the birthday of the church, the coming of the Holy Spirit, and the inauguration of a new age.

All things now are to become new. The way things have been are now to be changed to the way things should be. The weight of the past is now to give way to the liberation and enlightenment of the future.

Of course, it is not an accomplished fact, but an ongoing process toward a new day for the kingdom of God upon the earth. It is not a finished product, but a new reality being actualized in history by the inspiration of the Holy Spirit. Pentecost happened to those open to enlightenment by God and those open to God for the new age. It is always happening. It is hoped these sermons will be an aid toward those ends.

— Maurice A. Fetty

Table of Contents

Pentecost Day — 9
   Getting at the Truth
   John 14:8-17 (25-27)

Holy Trinity Sunday — 15
   Uncovering Cover-Ups
   John 16:12-15

Proper 4 — 23
Pentecost 2
Ordinary Time 9
   Finding Faith in Unlikely People
   Luke 7:1-10

Proper 5 — 31
Pentecost 3
Ordinary Time 10
   How to Rise Above Discouragement
   Luke 7:11-17

Proper 6 — 39
Pentecost 4
Ordinary Time 11
   The Challenge to Forgive
   Luke 7:36—8:3

Proper 7 — 47
Pentecost 5
Ordinary Time 12
   Demons, Pigs, and the Economy
   Luke 8:26-39

Proper 8   55
Pentecost 6
Ordinary Time 13
    Discipleship: Backward or Forward to God
    Luke 9:51-62

Proper 9   65
Pentecost 7
Ordinary Time 14
    How to Get the Job Done
    Luke 10:1-11, 16-20

Proper 10   73
Pentecost 8
Ordinary Time 15
    The Good Samaritan (Revised Edition)
    Luke 10:25-37

Proper 11   83
Pentecost 9
Ordinary Time 16
    Mary and Martha: Nine to Five and Five to Nine
    Luke 10:38-42

Proper 12   95
Pentecost 10
Ordinary Time 17
    Our Father Who Art in Heaven
    Luke 11:1-13

If You Like This Book...   105

Pentecost Day
John 14:8-17 (25-27)

Getting at the Truth

And I will pray the Father, and he will give you another counselor, to be with you forever, even the Spirit of truth, whom the world cannot receive, because it neither sees him nor knows him; you know him, for he dwells with you, and will be in you.
— John 14:16-17

The truth is hard to find these days. Perhaps it has been hard to find in any day. Do you remember ancient Diogenes who walked about with a lamp, shining it in men's faces, saying he was looking for an honest man? Diogenes felt he could never find a truthful person.

A little later in history Pontius Pilate reflected a similar skepticism, when at the trial of Jesus he asked cynically, "What is truth?" Anyone who has ever taken a few courses in philosophy will sympathize with Pilate.

If our Declaration of Independence begins by saying, "We hold these truths to be self-evident, that all men are created equal and are endowed by their Creator with certain inalienable rights," we who live under the Declaration 200 years later are not so sure all those truths are self-evident to everyone.

Truth is hard to find these days. Do you remember when President Jimmy Carter promised the American people he would never lie to us? We all knew, of course, that Nixon lied to us in the Watergate scandal. We had come to expect that most politicians, including presidents, lied to us regularly. So Carter's promise was met with sneering disbelief. If "read-my-lips-no-new-taxes" George H.W. Bush broke his promise, Bill Clinton, only four and one-half months into his presidency, broke at least three major campaign promises. Subsequent American presidents have been accused of deception and broken promises.

Truth is hard to find these days. We struggle with truth in advertising, truth in labeling, truth in packaging, as well as truth in medicine, law, business, and even religion. With such charlatans as Jimmy Bakker and Jimmy Swaggart, who deceived millions, even clergy men and women are more suspect than ever before. Truth is hard to find these days.

Even in families, truth is hard to find. Parents and children regularly deceive each other. Husbands and wives not only cheat on each other, they deceive each other with respect to true feelings. More than that, we often deceive ourselves. If Plato advised "know thyself," and if his teacher, Socrates, said the "unexamined life is not worth living," many of us are afraid really to examine ourselves too closely, or to come to know who we really are.

So truth is hard to find these days, partly because we do not want to find it. Yet it was Jesus who said, "I am the way, the truth, and the life." He said, "You will know the truth, and the truth will make you free." The Psalmist prayed, "Send out thy light and thy truth; let them lead me." In our text, Jesus promised he would send his Spirit of truth to teach and to comfort his people. It is the Holy Spirit that helps us get at the truth about ourselves and about our world.

I.

The Holy Spirit helps us get at the truth by teaching us the truth about reality.

At first, this must sound like another of the preposterous and propagandistic claims that are foisted on us today. More than that, many of us are more or less children of the enlightenment. Like our American founding fathers, we believe that truth is self-evident to the reasonable, rational mind. Along with philosopher John Locke, we think of truth as based on objective facts to be believed.

Yet, underlying these convictions is a deeper conviction that at the bottom of things, the world is orderly. The late Harvard mathematician and philosopher, Alfred North Whitehead, maintained that the whole scientific enterprise of the western world rested upon the belief that at the bottom of things science would find order rather than chaos. If animists were afraid to probe a world enchanted with demons and spirits, western scientists dissected, investigated, explored, and probed into the depths of the atom believing order and organization would be found rather than disorder and disarray.

What was at the bottom of the conviction? asked Whitehead. It was the theological concept of the Logos, the word or reason or mind of God, which held everything together. Why do things cohere and hold together? It is because the mind or Logos of God holds them together.

The early Christians, especially as represented in John's gospel, believed that the Logos or reason or mind of God became manifest in Jesus. Indeed, in his famous prologue to his gospel, John says that in Jesus, "the word (the Logos or reason of God) became flesh and dwelled among us, and we beheld his glory, the glory as of the only begotten of the Father, full of grace and truth" (1:14).

Earlier, John maintained this word (or Logos) was with God, was God, and was God's agent of creation. Thus, the Jesus of John's gospel can logically say, "Have I been so long with you Philip, and you did not know me? If you have seen me, you have seen the Father." So if Christ is a manifestation of the very word or reason or mind of God, Christ and his Spirit can lead us to the truth about reality.

What is that truth about ultimate reality Christ and his Spirit would have us know? It is that God is ultimate reality and that God is order, not chaos, and that God is love, not vindictive destructiveness. It is this conviction about ultimate reality that helps us probe the physical world as Harvard's Alfred North Whitehead maintained. It helps us believe that at bottom this world makes sense. There is purpose and life is not futile. Christ's Holy Spirit helps us get at the truth about ultimate reality.

II.

Christ's Holy Spirit also helps us get at the truth about our mental, spiritual, and psychological reality. We can probe the depths about ourselves believing order will prevail over chaos.

However, it is precisely here many of us get cold feet. Sometimes we are afraid to probe or to reveal ourselves fearing it will bring us harm. Men and women in competitive situations rarely confide in each other fearing the confidential information will be used against them to win the competitive edge. One married man told me he rarely confides in his wife or confesses to her any of his failings or weaknesses, because during arguments she uses that very information to berate him and tear him down.

However, other people have experienced something different. The twelve-step groups such as AA know that when they entrust their lives to a higher power and bare their souls to that power, they sense they are beginning to get in touch not only with themselves but with ultimate reality.

One young man told me about a small group of men from his church who meet once a week to share whatever is on their minds and hearts. They must agree to hold nothing back and to tell no one else what they have heard and shared. The young man said it has been a powerful, rewarding experience, helping him and others to come to the truth about themselves and reality.

Many of us, like Adam and Eve in the Garden of Eden, hide from God and from ourselves. We are fearful and defensive: fearful of too much self-knowledge that might require change, and defensive of our immature or immoral behavior that if known, might bring judgment and destruction.

The ultimate reality that Christ, the Logos, the reason or word of God, reveals is this: God is love and uses his judgment not to destroy but to purge, purify, and bring spiritual health. If we let him, the Holy Spirit will bring us to the truth about ourselves and ultimate reality.

III.

Lastly, the Holy Spirit of Christ helps us get the truths about ourselves to God.

When John's gospel speaks of the Holy Spirit, it speaks of the comforter, counselor, or advocate. The Greek word used by John is *paraclete*, which comes from a word meaning "to call alongside." A paraclete is one we call alongside us, to be with us, to be our advocate when we seem powerless to advocate for ourselves.

One of my church members told of an extended stay in a hospital. She was lamenting the rather poor service and considerable inattention to detail. Thankfully, she was able to afford a private duty nurse to be her advocate. Otherwise, many of her needs would have been neglected. Most all of us feel we need an advocate or counselor at law. The ombudsman has come into popularity to represent people who are powerless with businesses or bureaucracies. Many of us belong to various kinds of advocacy groups which aid us in the presence of complex issues and powerful forces.

The Holy Spirit of Christ is just such an advocate. Jesus has called him to our side to be our counselor and comforter. When we approach almighty God, we have an advocate, because as Paul says, "The Spirit helps us in our weakness;

for we do not know how to pray as we ought, but the Spirit himself intercedes for us with sighs too deep for words. And he who searches the hearts of men knows what is the mind of the Spirit, because the Spirit intercedes for the saints according to the will of the Father" (Romans 8:26-27).

In other words, not only does the Spirit help us get at the truth about ourselves, it helps God understand the truth or reality about our situation. If the Spirit is a channel of God's reality to humanity, it is also a channel of humanity's reality to God. The Spirit pleads our case before the almighty, and Christ himself, says the epistle to the Hebrews, sits at the right hand of the Father, making eternal intercession for all humanity (Hebrews 7:25).

If the world in its darkness and immorality is afraid to come to the light, to the truth, because its deeds are evil, we need not be afraid to do so. We are brave enough to explore and probe the world, believing order prevails over chaos.

We are brave enough to try to get at the elusive truth about ourselves, believing if we confess our sins, God is willing to forgive our wrongs and hurtful words and actions.

Perhaps most encouraging of all is the assurance that the Spirit represents our truth before God — the truth of our disease and pain, the truth of our tragedy and despair, the truth of injustice and exploitation, the truth of depression and death. The Spirit of Christ is our paraclete, our advocate and counselor, assuring us that God is not chaos and destruction, but order and love. We give thanks that the Holy Spirit helps us get at these essential truths. Amen.

Holy Trinity Sunday
John 16:12-15

Uncovering Cover-Ups

When the Spirit of truth comes, he will guide you into all the truth. — John 16:13

For some it is ancient history. But for others it is as fresh as yesterday. I speak of 1972 when the word "cover-up" came into our consciousness in a big way — the cover-up by then-President Richard Nixon regarding the Watergate scandal.

Assured of a landslide victory in his election for a second term, Richard Nixon, overborne with anxiety, apparently felt that was not enough. So he authorized the so-called "Watergate Plumbers," headed by G. Gordon Liddy, to break into the Democratic Headquarters in the posh Washington DC Watergate apartment complex.

Bungling the third-rate burglary job, the "plumbers" were found to be connected to Republican officials higher and higher up in the administration, until the press was pointing its powerful fingers at President Nixon himself. Wasn't he involved in authorizing the Watergate burglary? Not so, said the president.

Then it became known that the Oval Office had an elaborate tape recording system where all conversations were recorded. Was there evidence, asked the special prosecutor, was there evidence on the tapes that Nixon had authorized the break in? Eventually, through court order, the tapes (later published as The Presidential Transcripts) were turned over but with eighteen crucial minutes of recorded voices missing.

15

The pressure mounted on President Nixon. More and more people, especially the press, believed he was involved. Many implicated him in the crime and said he was doing his best to "stonewall" and cover-up the authorization of his law breaking. Thus the one sworn to uphold the Constitution was believed to have violated his oath. Under threat of impeachment, President Nixon resigned his office in 1973, turning over the presidency to Gerald Ford, Congressman from Grand Rapids, Michigan. The cover-up had been uncovered.

Since that time, we have had no shortage of exposures of cover-ups and as a result, the image of some of our dearest heroes has been tarnished. For example, my father and his generation were great admirers of J. Edgar Hoover, head of the F.B.I. But many books and articles on Hoover have uncovered a variety of behavior and improprieties that would have greatly offended my dad.

President John F. Kennedy lauded Thomas Jefferson when, at an assemblage of artists, actors, authors, and musicians in the East Room of the White House, he remarked that there probably had never been such a gathering of talent in the East Room, except possibly when Thomas Jefferson dined alone. Yet recent books have suggested improprieties in Jefferson's behavior, such as allegedly retaining a black slave woman as mistress by whom he allegedly fathered several children.

The Reverend Martin Luther King Jr., led a civil rights revolution in this country in the '60s. He had a dream of the day when prejudice and discrimination would end and we would dwell together as one people. He was a nonviolent advocate of morality, integrity, virtue, truthfulness, and justice. Yet recent books have claimed he was a womanizer and that he plagiarized a significant part of his doctoral thesis. The cover-up was uncovered.

Is it any wonder this is happening? It is precisely what Jesus predicted and promised to his disciples. The Holy Spirit, the Spirit of truth, will come and will expose the deeds of all people, making known even the thoughts and intents of the heart. This divine Spirit he would send from the Father will convict the world of sin, righteousness, and judgment. The Spirit will uncover what is covered up.

I.

Consider the first matter of sin.

Some years ago when Senator Estes Kefauver was heading up his famous Senate committee investigating mobs and racketeering, he exposed many scandals, rackets, and corrupt politicians and business people. One day during the hearings, one mobster testifying said, "Everybody's doing what we're doing. Why don't you just stop all this nonsense and call everything legal?"

Why not indeed! The mobster was not too far off from the popular mood that denies any ultimate sense of right and wrong. For many people there are no moral absolutes, no divine commandments to be obeyed, no universal, timeless principles to which they feel obligated. Many people are governed by whatever gives them pleasure or satisfies their lust, ambition, or craving for power and notoriety. "Do your own thing so long as it doesn't hurt anybody" is the popular slogan. If it gives you pleasure or makes you happy, it's okay.

The late Chuck Colson, founder of Prison Fellowship and recipient of the coveted 1993 Templeton Prize in Religion, will be remembered by many as President Nixon's rough and tough "hatchet man." Now a remarkable "born-again" Christian and tireless worker for prison reformation, Colson says that our culture has "spent the last several years determined to secularize our society." We live, says Colson, "in a culture in which we sit and watch, hour by hour, the banality that passes for knowledge on television, and we rarely think about issues in terms of the Judeo-Christian truth" (*Imprimis*, Hillsdale College, April 1993).

Colson asked in his speech given at Hillsdale College, Hillsdale, Michigan, "Can we be good without God?" His resounding answer is "no." Any society, especially a free society, says Colson, "depends on a moral consensus and on shared assumptions.... These common values are the glue that hold society together." But we have had an erosion of these values and shared assumptions, says Colson. We are reminded of ancient Israel in a time without king or law when everyone did what was right in his own eyes with ensuing corruption and chaos.

Take heart, says Jesus in our text. The Holy Spirit will be with you to convict the world of sin and of right and wrong. The Spirit of truth will manifest itself through my witnesses to call right right and wrong wrong.

And that is precisely what is happening through courageous, committed spokesmen like Charles Colson. That is precisely what is happening in thousands of religious communities all across this land and the world. We remain convinced there is a right in the world and a wrong. Everything is not dissolved into amoral relativism.

II.

If the divine Spirit convicts the world of sin, it also convicts of righteousness and justice.

The pastoral letters of the New Testament urge church people not to become weary in well-doing. But over the long haul, in the battle against injustice and unrighteousness, we wonder, in the words of Shakespeare, if love's labor is lost. Will darkness overcome light? Will the weeds win over the beautiful blossoms and nutritious plants?

That question has grown to monumental proportions in our society with the breakdown of families, the high incidence of physical and sexual abuse, and the abuse of alcohol and drugs. It has been reported that some parents actually encourage keg parties for their teenagers, and that others even rent hotel suites and stock them with liquor for their teenagers and their parties.

Perhaps even more alarming is the sharp rise in teenage crime and violence. For example, Chuck Colson in the early 1990s pointed out that in Washington DC, "46% of the inner city black population between the ages of 18 and 21 is either in prison, on parole, or on probation." Let's say that again — that's nearly half the inner city blacks in our nation's capital.

Colson says we have the highest per capita rate of incarceration in the world. Our prisons are bursting their seams. In the last several years murders committed by those between the ages of 18 and 20 have increased 120%. He quotes some sources that claim 20% of all school children carry a gun.

Time magazine had a cover story titled "A Boy and His Gun." Youngsters today are buying and using guns at an alarming rate, says the article. Even in Omaha, Nebraska, in the heartland where it might be thought family values and morals would prevail — even in Omaha, gun possession and use are widespread.

One of the boys interviewed had in four months done nine drive-by shootings aiming mostly at houses and cars. He killed a dog for no reason at all and his brother missed a baby's head by a quarter of an inch. Is it any wonder that many teenagers are killed by guns?

Many of the gun-toting youngsters interviewed came from families that were messed up in some way or other. Many seem to shoot and kill with no remorse or guilt. A terrible amorality seems to prevail. The gun seems to represent protection and macho power. It also, says the *Time* reporter, represents a "defense against the inexplicable despair that torments so many American teenagers. Today's miscreants know that a pistol says much more than long hair or a pierced nose ever could. Not just louder but forever. With a $25 investment, all the teasing from classmates stops cold. Suddenly, the shortest, ugliest, and weakest kid becomes a player" (*Time*, August 2, 1993, p. 23). Consequently, kids, like nations, come to believe with Chairman Mao that morality begins at the muzzle of a gun.

Yet, this Holy Spirit of God is uncovering this cover-up of his eternal truth. A group of parents has organized to counteract the violence. They meet each night to pray and then to patrol the streets to ward off violence and keep kids from shooting one another.

So long as there are groups like that, so long as there are churches and religious people standing up for nonviolence and decency, so long as there are people working for gun control and social responsibility — so long as these and many other things take place, the Holy Spirit is convicting the world for righteousness' sake and love's labor is not lost. Let no one cover up that.

III.

Lastly, Jesus says his Holy Spirit of truth will convict the world of judgment.

At first hearing, most all of us don't like that word "judgment." We immediately think of self-righteous people being uppity and censorious. We have images of holier-than-thou types who look down on us with disdain, or of social snobs who have kept us out of their clubs or social circles. Convinced that most everyone has a character flaw covered up somewhere, we resent the thought of anyone judging us for anything.

We quickly justify our feeling by quoting Jesus' famous saying in the Sermon on the Mount, "judge not lest you be judged," or again, his saying that we ought first to cast out the wooden beam in our own eye before we try to remove the sawdust from our brother's or sister's eye.

The judgment referred to here is the divine judgment: the divine judgment that is absolutely fair and impartial, the divine judgment that cannot be seduced or bribed, the divine judgment that finally and forever makes full disclosure of the truth. The scripture says, let God be found true and every man a liar.

When the truth is known, we all realize the cover-ups in our lives. Many of us fear the truth. We do not want to be exposed to the light because our deeds are evil. Most of us have something about our lives we do not want exposed to anyone. If the truth be known, could we bear to live with one another?

Let's ask the question differently. If the truth can never be known, or if there is no truth, no truth at all, does anything make any difference at all? Isn't life then a tale told by an idiot, full of sound and fury, signifying nothing?

It is precisely this futility, this relativism, this aimlessness and despair that the divine Spirit promises to overcome. The Holy Spirit's witness in the world through the church is testimony to the fact that things do make a difference, life is going somewhere, and our lives do have meaning and sacred value.

The fact that there is a judgment, an accounting, means that there is a goal line, a degree to be granted at the end of the course, a reward to be received, a meaningful culmination of all our labors. If parents exercise no judgment, their children rightly perceive they are indifferent and have no guiding values. If God exercises no judgment, we might rightly perceive him to be indifferent and even non-existent.

This is a text of hopefulness. There is judgment because God cares. He uncovers the cover-ups, not to destroy us, but to bring us to the light so that we might be healthy and flourish.

The sin and evil of the world attempt to squelch truth and justice and purpose. But take heart, says Jesus, because the divine Spirit will be with you always to uncover the cover-ups so that you might be healthy and whole. Amen.

**Proper 4
Pentecost 2
Ordinary Time 9
Luke 7:1-10**

Finding Faith in Unlikely People

When Jesus heard this he marveled at him, and turned and said to the multitudes that followed him, "I tell you, not even in Israel have I found such faith." — Luke 7:9

One of the continuing delights of life is the joy of the unexpected. Tightly scheduled as we are, and rigorously regimented, occasionally we are extraordinarily pleased with interruption and variation. When out-of-town friends turn up unannounced, rather than having scheduled themselves weeks in advance, we experience a certain excitement. How pleasant to have a business deal grow to undreamed proportions. What joy in having a surprise verdict from judge and jury. What a thrill to see surgery and medication do far more than expected. Thankfully, life has innumerable surprises.

Our text centers on Jesus' surprise at finding faith in an unlikely person. He expected his fellow Israelites to be responsive to his word. They shared with him a common heritage and faith, a regularized way of seeing and thinking.

But a Roman centurion was something else! Who would expect to find a sincere faith in him? He was a man of authority and power. Not only was he an outsider, he represented the hated enemy. A man of talent and intelligence, the centurion of Capernaum believed nevertheless. Jesus could not contain his delight at this unexpected discovery of faith in an unlikely person. "I tell you," he said, "nowhere, even in Israel, have I found faith like this" (v. 9).

I.

One unlikely place we find faith is in people of authority and power — unlikely because we assume power and faith are mutually exclusive. The more powerful you are the less you need faith — or so we sometimes say.

Notice on the one hand this view holds religion to be mainly a crutch for the weak and cowardly. It serves as a kind of divine apron string behind which we can safely view the ordeals of the world. It sees faith as a sop for the superstitious, a hiding place for the timid.

One problem with this view is the fallacious presumption man needs no outside help, that he can, if he will, stand on his own two feet without psychological crutches and canes. Where do you find a man like that, one who lives without support of any kind? In the 1960s it was popular to write of man coming of age, the secular man, a sort of deified playboy — sophisticated, cool, worldly wise, self-contained, self-sufficient, reserved, independent, a connoisseur of wines and women, a distinguished man among men who had his head together, who was never fooled or taken. This 1960s man coming of age never sinned, though he might have made errors in judgment because he didn't have all the facts. Consequently, he claimed no guilt, was oblivious to remorse and regret, and viewed the world as the survival of the fittest. Most assuredly he was fit and he was surviving.

Or was he really? Carrying some of these attitudes into the 1970s we had a president who, through the cynical and criminal use of power, wreaked havoc on careers and reputations and assaulted with cool contempt the institutions and principles, which give this nation some of its uniqueness. Tough, cool, calculating, our man at the top, embodying for many the ideal man coming of age, believed power was the whole name of the game. Power. Period. Nothing more. Get before you are gotten, strike before you are stricken, push before you are pushed, destroy before you are destroyed. And still no public admission of guilt. It's one thing to make mistakes; it's quite another to sin against the foundations of a democracy. The so-called modern secular man doesn't need a crutch, doesn't need anything to hold him up. But irony of ironies, even Achilles has a vulnerable heel.

Or consider another manifestation of the power and authority mentality: money. Some time ago I had the pleasure of hearing an independent press correspondent speak. He gave interesting insights into the world situation. Money is the name of the game, he said. All international disputes are reducible to money.

But not quite. Of course economic matters play a huge role in world peace. Unquestionably, wars are fought over money and its power. But to reduce everything to money and money making is an over simplification.

The correspondent went on to speak of the ongoing Mid-East disputes. Who do they want to arbitrate the disputes? Frequently it is America because it is often believed America will be fair and compassionate.

So power and money are not the whole name of the game in international relations. Fairness and compassion enter in. Brutality is counter-balanced with gentleness and consideration for the other point of view. Power isn't the whole name of the game. Rather it is the conviction that human life is sacred, even human life that is weak and faltering, in need of someone to lean on.

Note another aspect of power and authority. The centurion who came to Jesus was not only willing to confess his need of help, but he also recognized the derivative sources of power. In other words, he knew ultimately that power and authority came from outside himself. He recognized himself as a channel, a distributor of power.

He saw Jesus in a similar role. The centurion commanded soldiers in the name of Caesar; Jesus commanded spirits in the name of God. They each saw themselves as channels of higher power and authority. As Jesus said, "I can do nothing on my own authority... because I seek not my own will but the will of him who sent me" (John 5:30). At his trial Pilate derided Jesus, saying, "You will not speak to me? Do you not know that I have power to release you, and power to crucify you?" Jesus answered him, "You would have no power over me unless it had been given you from above..." (John 19:10-11). Pilate believed his power came from Caesar. Jesus knew Caesar's power came from God, as did his own. All power is derivative and finally it is derived from God.

Governmental cynics see America's power as derived from missiles, planes, guns, aircraft carriers, the Pentagon, and institutions of government. Actually, America's strength is derived from the consent of the governed, and the consent of the governed is founded upon principles and ideals that have divine origins.

Cynics see legal power as derived from lawmakers, lawyers, and the judiciary. But all laws rest squarely on the will of the people, and the will of the people rests on principles, values, and ideals that are divine in origin. Ultimately, man's law rests upon the law of God. Likewise medicine rests upon the power of healing, which comes from God. All power is derivative power.

The temptation of man is to believe he has done it all by himself, he is sufficient unto himself, and he has originated his own power. That is why Jesus was delighted to see a man of authority have such depth of understanding. He found faith in God in an unlikely person. Does he find it in us?

II.

Jesus was also surprised to find faith in the centurion because he was an outsider and an enemy. He expected his insider friends to have faith but not his outsider enemy.

One of the persistent surprises in biblical history is God's use of the outsider. Joseph was thrown out by his brothers and sold into slavery, but God used him to change history. In Egypt, the Hebrews were outsiders and slaves, but God freed them and gave them their own land. Moses was meek and poor at making speeches, yet God used him as the leader. David was the youngest and unlikeliest of Jesse's sons, yet God made him king. Amos was neither a prophet nor the son of a prophet, yet his message became God's message. Cyrus, the conquering Persian king, is called God's messiah by Isaiah. Jesus himself was scorned as an outsider northerner by the elitist southern circle of pretenders to the throne. "Can anything good come out of Nazareth?" (the north) they asked sneeringly.

Drawing on the universalism of some of the great prophets, Jesus taught that God was not the exclusive possession of the chosen people. He knew what Isaiah meant when he said: "See, they come; some from far away, these from the north and these from the west and these from the land of Syene" (Isaiah 49:12 NEB). He was acquainted with Malachi's prophecy: "From furthest east to furthest west my name is great among the nations" (Malachi 1:11 NEB).

While Jesus may have begun his ministry with a rather exclusivistic view of God as Israel's exclusive possession, he soon expanded his vision to behold the amazing work of God throughout the world, even to the Romans — the enemies. What a breakthrough. Heretofore, with the exception of some of the prophets, God was seen as a national deity. The Jews were not alone in this belief. Most nations had their special god or gods. He was theirs exclusively and devoted his divine powers to gaining victories and prosperity for them.

The great Israelite prophets saw that God sometimes used outsiders to bring repentance. The prophet Amos in

741 BC warned Israel that God would use the Assyrians to punish them if they did not repent. They did not repent and in 721 BC the Assyrians did indeed destroy the Israelite nation, exiling many of the people and resettling outsiders in the land.

Jeremiah of Jerusalem warned the southern nation of Judah that if they did not repent, God would use the Babylonians to punish them. They did not repent and in 587 BC the Babylonians did indeed invade Judah, destroying Jerusalem and the grand temple of Solomon. God sometimes uses the outsider "enemy" to carry out his purposes. Sometimes faith is found in unlikely people and places.

Often America has had the too-easy assumption that God is on our side and that he always will give us victory and prosperity because we stand for righteousness, truth, and morality. Freedom is God's aim for man, and since America extols and celebrates freedom, God will always spare her — or so we think.

As Jesus observed long ago, "Many, I tell you will come from east and west to feast with Abraham, Isaac and Jacob in the kingdom of heaven. But those who were born to the kingdom will be driven out into the dark, the place of wailing and grinding of teeth" (Matthew 8:11-12). It is not a matter of being an insider, said Jesus, not a matter of ecclesiastical aristocracy or religious pedigree, but a matter of faith — faith that is open and possible for all.

III.

Notice further that Jesus was surprised with the Centurion's faith in his word. The Centurion may have had some opportunity to be exposed to the wisdom of Rome and Greece. Undoubtedly he was sharp and capable. Yet he was teachable and ready to believe what Jesus had to say.

Often the assumption is that the more intelligent you are and the more you know, the less faith you need. Faith often is regarded as the instrument of the credulous and feeble-minded. For those who are truly enlightened, who are really in the know, faith is superfluous or so the argument sometimes goes. Knowing this, Jesus was delighted to find faith in a man who might have regarded himself as intellectually sophisticated.

One of the sins of Jesus' contemporaries was the belief they had it all in the bag, and God had given them his complete revelation and knowledge of himself. It was that very belief that closed them off to the new thing that was happening in their midst.

> *Woe to you, Chorazin! Woe to you, Bethsaida! For if the mighty works done in you had been done in Tyre and Sidon, they would have repented long ago in sack cloth and ashes... And you, Capernaum, will you be exalted to heaven? You shall be brought down to Hades. For if the mighty works done in you had been done in Sodom, it would have remained until this day. But I tell you that it shall be more tolerable on the day of judgment for the land of Sodom than for you.*
> — Matthew 11:21-24

The outsiders were more receptive to the truth than the insiders. Consequently Jesus prayed, "I thank thee, Father, Lord of heaven and earth, that thou hast hidden these things from the wise and understanding and revealed them to babes; yea, Father, for such was thy gracious will" (Matthew 11:25-26). A childlike openness is necessary to receive new truth. Very often our sophisticated intellectualisms prevent us from seeing the new truth trying to break in upon us. Regrettably, education sometimes causes us to be arrogant and blasé, whereas it should awaken humility and wonder.

As Elizabeth Barrett Browning wrote:

> Earth's crammed with heaven
> And every bush afire with God.
> But only he who sees takes off his shoes.
> The rest sit round it, and pluck blackberries
> *And daub their natural faces unaware.*
> — *The Treasury of Religious Verse* (ed. Donald T. Kauffman [Fleming Revell, 1966], p. 11)

As the New Testament scholars Major, Manson, and Wright have written, "The window lets in the light, but not the blind. It reveals the wide-stretching landscape, but not if we close our eyes.... The whole universe is sacramental, but only if we are spiritually awake" (*The Mission and Message of Jesus*, p. 692). The centurion, outsider that he was, had his eyes open. He was spiritually aware. Whereas the insiders, the religious types, were puffed up with intellectual pride and blinded with the cataracts of conceit.

Irony of ironies, surprise of surprises — the outsiders are in, the insiders are out; the wise are humbled, the humble are made wise; the powerful are made weak, the weak are made powerful; the righteous became sinners, the sinners became righteous; the first are last, and the last are first. Faith is found in unlikely people. Amen.

Proper 5
Pentecost 3
Ordinary Time 10
Luke 7:11-17

How to Rise Above Discouragement

And he came and touched the bier, and the bearers stood still. And he said "Young man, I say to you, arise." And the dead man sat up, and began to speak. And he gave him to his mother.
— Luke 7:14-15

It's a dramatic scene when you think about it — a funeral procession halted and the trip to the cemetery interrupted. Of course it was not anything like our scene — a black Cadillac hearse, followed by one or more black Cadillac limousines, followed perhaps by several cars, lights on, concerned not to lose their place in the line in the traffic.

This scene was at once more primitive and personal. No city traffic to contend with in this procession. No indifferent motorists disturbed that they are delayed a few minutes because of the funeral. No, this is a village scene — people on foot, following the widowed mother, who is following the professional mourners with their cymbals, flutes, and high-pitched shrieking and wailing. It is a Palestinian village scene in Nain, just a short distance from Nazareth, Jesus' hometown, and a day's walk from Capernaum, Jesus' new adopted town.

The pallbearers are carrying the body of a young man in a long wicker basket covered by a shroud for burial outside the city. Ancient Jews buried their dead outside the city, usually on the day of death or the next day because embalming was not practiced.

For modern, indifferent eyes and blasé people, the scene was dramatic enough by itself. Think of it: the dead man was the only son of his mother, and she was a widow. The pathos and sorrow of the ages is contained in that statement, for in a patriarchal society orphans, of which he was one, and widows, which she was, were regarded as vulnerable, weak, and without much opportunity for economic support. Nonetheless, a great crowd followed the procession, indicating sympathy and support at least for the time being.

That's drama enough — a large crowd of caring people — but now there is more. Jesus approaches, apparently coming from Capernaum where he just healed the Roman centurion's slave. He saw the widowed, desolate mother, had compassion for her, and thought perhaps of his own mother reputedly widowed at an early age.

"Do not weep," he told her, her tears for her son no doubt now intermingling with the endless salty tears shed for her husband. In the continuing drama, risking ceremonial impurity, he reached out, touched the bier and possibly the body, and the procession halted.

Can you see the modern setting? Someone halting the hearse, opening the door of the limousine, telling the widowed mother in the black attire of mourning not to weep, and then saying beside the coffin, "Young man, I say to you arise." Startling indeed, and startling enough in first-century Palestine which had a tradition of miracle stories of great prophets like Elijah and Elisha raising widows' sons from the dead. The young man sat up and began to speak, and like Elijah and Elisha before Jesus, the new great prophet gave the son back to his mother.

Talk about rising above discouragement! Talk about overcoming the greatest obstacle to human fulfillment. Talk about overcoming life's defeats, this was it — Jesus raising this young man from the dead as he had Jairus' daughter and Lazarus, brother of Mary and Martha.

He didn't raise everybody physically from the dead, of course, just as he didn't heal everybody. What he did do then and still does today is to help everyone rise above discouragement. That's where we focus today — rising above discouragement.

I.

How do we rise above discouragement? For one thing we do not deny the reality of our trouble.

Biblical scholar William Barclay says, "We live in a world of broken hearts." Indeed we do. Any daily newspaper recounts tragic story after tragic story of premature deaths, fractured relationships, and broken dreams. Indeed, we need not turn to any newspaper for an accounting of the world's troubles and sorrows. We have only to look at our own friends, neighbors, and families. We have only to look into our own lives and hearts.

Jesus, the healer and power giver, never insulted people by telling them their problems weren't real. He never told the sick they were not really sick or that their illness had no pain or reality. He never told people that death wasn't real. He did not offer this widowed mother Pollyannaish pablum to soothe her grieving heart.

I am reminded of a friend living in Indiana where tornadoes are frequent. His young son had a special fear of storms. One day, when a storm threatened, the father took his son to the front door of their home, pointed out across the neighborhood, and said to the boy, "There, you see, everything is okay. These are solid homes and we are safe and dry in them."

About that time a tornado touched down a block away and utterly destroyed several of those homes. The storms of the natural world are real just as are the storms of the spiritual, psychological world. Trouble and tragedy are real. Evil and death are real. Jesus never said to his disciples on the stormy Sea of Galilee, "This is no storm. The storm is in your mind." He never said that. Instead he said to the storm, "Peace be still." And it was.

Are you out of a job? Did your home decline in value? Are your financial resources dwindling? Do you have a serious illness? Is your marriage not right? Is there a real problem with the children? Are you enslaved in a debilitating habit? Then don't deny it, says Jesus. The widow never said her son wasn't dead. Admit the problems. Don't deny them. That's the first step in overcoming discouragement.

II.

How are we to rise above discouragement? We need the courage to consider alternatives.

A few years ago I was counseling a woman in a troubled marriage. Over the course of several counseling sessions she recited in great detail the woes of her marriage and the faults and foibles of her spouse. The problems were real and she was indeed an unhappy woman.

When it came to considering alternatives, she was closed-minded. Her husband was abusive and would not, under any circumstances, consider counseling. Why not get a separation or divorce, I asked. She couldn't for the sake of their child. The child is almost grown and gone and besides he thinks you should get out of the relationship, I said.

She then stated she could not afford to move out. "But," I said, "you already are gainfully employed, and from what you have told me, earn quite a good income."

"But," she replied, "without his income I would have to live at a lower level than that to which I have become accustomed." And so it went. She was indeed very unhappy in the marriage and had been for a long time. She was very discouraged, even to the point of despair, and perhaps even flirted once in a while with the thought of suicide. Yet she refused seriously to consider any alternative to her current situation.

Here is a man about to lose his job due to large lay-offs in his company. He has two cars, a large mortgage, kids in school, and one in college. The job market is tough, but his company does help him in outplacement. However, it is in an area of the country that is not as appealing and is some distance from his mother and father, on whom he is quite psychologically dependent. So he turns down the outplacement and is faced with probable personal bankruptcy. He's greatly discouraged, but is so in large measure because he refused seriously to consider real alternatives.

I see this over and over again. People come to a dead end in marriage, job, or self-understanding and then refuse to consider alternatives. They often refuse to consider alternatives because they want the future to be just like the past. They are afraid of adjustment or change. They have forgotten the words to James Russell Lowell's famous hymn:

New occasions teach new duties,
Time makes ancient good uncouth.
He must always up and onward,
Who would keep abreast of truth.
— *Pilgrim Hymnal* (Pilgrim Press: Boston, 1962, "Once to Every Man and Nation")

Long before Lowell it was Jesus who told the sick to have faith, stand up, and walk. It was Jesus who said to the blind man, do you want to see? The man answered that he did. It was Jesus who said, take up your cross and follow me. It was Jesus who said, if you have faith you can move mountains. It was Jesus himself who refused to be defeated by circumstances. Instead, he considered alternative ways of thinking and acting. That's what made him such a revolutionary person.

Want to rise above discouragement? Then let go of the past, the dead ends, the cul-de-sacs, the corners you've painted yourself into, and consider the alternatives Christ is ready to show you.

III.

How do we rise above discouragement? We must allow ourselves to be touched by Christ, by the transcendent, by the divine reality that is greater than ourselves.

One of the surest ways to discouragement and death is to assume that all reality begins and ends with you. An acquaintance believes if she hasn't thought it, it isn't true; or if she hasn't experienced it, it hasn't happened. The whole of reality is therefore defined by her narrow perceptions.

The late Jacob Bronowski, outstanding scientist with the Salk Institute, illustrated that truth in the world of science. He did a popular television series he later turned into a book titled *The Ascent of Man*. This book chronicled the development of scientific knowledge and understanding.

In the chapter having to do with knowledge and certainty, Bronowski confessed and lamented how arrogant science had at one time become. He said he remembered when scientists thought they were on the verge of discovering the key to all reality, when suddenly a new discovery would open up a whole new world, and reality would lurch away from them into infinity. He then added we should avoid all arrogant, dogmatic stances with respect to knowledge and say in the words of Oliver Cromwell, "I beseech you, in the bowels of Christ, think it possible you may be mistaken" (*The Ascent of Man* [Little, Brown and Company, 1973], p. 374).

Invariably, when people become discouraged, they have allowed their own world and self-understanding to collapse in around them. Many discouraged and despairing people are suffocating in their own conceit. They get caught in the grip of doubt and refuse to doubt their own doubts — they refuse to question their own stale definitions of self and reality.

In contrast to this, Jesus calls us to open up to the divine in prayer and humility. Even yesteryear's skeptic, Thomas Huxley, said the longer he lived, he thought one of man's most sacred acts is to say "I believe." Harry Emerson Fosdick the famous preacher of Riverside Church, New York City, came to a similar conclusion. Called to pastor and build that big church backed by the Rockefeller family and fortune, Fosdick eventually had a nervous breakdown.

Fosdick said the nervous breakdown was the most terrifying wilderness he ever traveled through. He wanted to commit suicide, but instead made some of the most vital discoveries of his life. He said he found God in a desert, and out of that experience came his influential book *The Meaning of Prayer*. Fosdick came to say "I believe" in a new and vital way.

We are forever learning that God is for us, not against us. It is we who are against ourselves in our myopia, our rigidity, our fear, our arrogance and stubbornness. Many of us are slow learners. We refuse to allow God to touch us with the new idea, the new self-understanding, the new job, the new opportunity, the new vital power he has to give.

It was Isaiah the prophet who put it so well for the Lord:

> *Seek the Lord while he may be found, call upon him while he is near... For my thoughts are not your thoughts, neither are your ways my ways, says the Lord. For as the heavens are higher than the earth, so are my ways higher than your ways and my thoughts than your thoughts.* — Isaiah 55:6, 8-9

It was the divine power that spoke to the dead young man that day long ago in the village of Nain. It was a dramatic sight, a rarity with Elijah, Elisha, Jesus, and perhaps a few other great prophets. We shall have to wait until the end of time to see the grand resurrection of the dead.

But in our time and in all time, the power of the living Christ raises people up from discouragement, despondency, despair, and from death itself. The Bible and books of the world and the churches are full of stories of how God helped and helps people rise above discouragement. As Jesus said to that young man in Nain long ago, so would he say to each of us today, "Young man or old, young woman or old, I say to you, arise." And you will. Amen.

**Proper 6
Pentecost 4
Ordinary Time 11
Luke 7:36—8:3**

The Challenge to Forgive

Therefore I tell you, her sins, which are many, are forgiven, for she loved much; but he who is forgiven little, loves little.
— Luke 7:47

It is a dramatic scene out of America's mythical past — a Western scene of cowboys, saloons, and gunslingers; a scene of wide-open spaces conquered by fierce individualists, liquor, and true grit. It is a scene, however, a little different from the cowboy heroes of my childhood, the scenes of the good guy, white hat heroes like Roy Rogers and Gene Autry, not even to mention the good guy, white hat hero horses like Trigger or Silver of the Lone Ranger's "Hi, Ho Silver, away!"

Yes, it is a scene unlike my childhood memories of cowboys and Indians and the Lone Ranger and his faithful Indian sidekick Tonto. The scene is more in keeping with today's Lone Ranger episode where the famous good guy lawman and Tonto are being charged by a vicious group of Indians. "Looks like we have a problem, Tonto," said the Long Ranger. And Tonto replied, "What do you mean *we*, white man!"

Yes, this is the tougher, harsher, gutsier scene of murder and mayhem, violence and killing, where the bad guys, if they don't win, at least don't seem to lose. I speak of the scenes in the award-winning movie, *Unforgiven*, starring Clint Eastwood as Bill Munny, who was "a known thief and murderer, a man of notoriously vicious and intemperate disposition." However, he married, and it is his gentle wife who bears him two children and leads him into a settled and reformed, if impoverished, life where he hangs up his six guns to raise pigs.

His wife's untimely death from small pox crippled him on his road to recovery from his addiction to violence. And so does the arrival of a young gunslinger, the Schofield Kid. The Kid announces a handsome reward has been offered by two prostitutes if someone will kill the two men who beat them badly and cut one of them. Eastwood, as ex-sharpshooter killer Bill Munny, cannot resist. Looking at the thin faces of his poverty-stricken children, he decides to go after the reward for their sake. He decides to kill to give them a better life.

Bill Munny takes along Ned, his old killing partner, and the two of them, along with the Schofield Kid, shoot their way into town, shoot the prostitute-abusing cowboys, shoot their way out of the saloon, and Munny eventually shoots the sheriff, who lies wounded on the saloon floor.

The sheriff says to Munny, "I don't deserve this. I was building a house." Munny responds, "Deserves got nothing to do with this." The sheriff defiantly replies, "I'll see you in hell, William Munny." "Yes," Munny agrees, as he kills him. All the work of Munny's late wife toward his reformation and forgiveness was undone. Tragically, at the movie's end, violent and murderous as ever, he remains *un*forgiven.

Our text for today from Luke's gospel also involves a prostitute — a prostitute some 1,800 years previous to those in the movie. And unlike the prostitutes in the movie who are seeking revenge, the prostitute in the biblical story is seeking forgiveness and an opportunity to express gratitude. In contrast to the movie, the tragedy of violence and death is turned into the triumph of forgiveness and reconciliation.

One time a minister was giving a children's sermon. The topic was forgiveness. He asked the children, "What must we do to receive forgiveness?" One little boy raised his hand and said, "Well first of all we have to sin!" Or as one well-intentioned woman said to her new minister upon leaving worship after the sermon, "I must tell you, Reverend, we never really knew what sin was until you came."

Sin and forgiveness are at the heart of the church's vocabulary. Indeed, the word *sin* occurs 446 times in the Bible. When one minister announced in a Sunday sermon that there were over 285 different kinds of sin mentioned in the Bible, on Monday his secretary was flooded with calls asking for a detailed list!

Even though the word *forgive*, and its cognates appear only about 150 times in the Bible, the concept of forgiveness is even more central to the Bible than the concept of sin. If sin is the eternal enticement of humankind, the eternal yearning of humanity is for forgiveness, and our eternal challenge is to be able to forgive. Just how do we go about forgiving?

I.

The first step in the challenge to forgive is to accept forgiveness for ourselves.

Many scholars, commentators, and ministers often have alluded to psychiatrist Karl Menninger's popular book, *Whatever Became of Sin?* Dr. Menninger, the founder of the well-known Menninger Clinic in Topeka, Kansas, gave a series of lectures at Princeton that were expanded into this attention getting book.

Throughout the book, Menninger observes that most Americans believe many things are tragically wrong and that there is a lot of sin and badness out there. Corruption and dishonesty are rampant, hypocrisy and duplicity abound, fraud and scam schemes are everywhere, our society is in deplorable moral disrepair, and on and on.

But, says Dr. Menninger, despite all this societal breast-beating, no one ever admits to doing any wrong. People bemoaning the many sins and corruptions of America do not see themselves as corrupt sinners. People lament the decay in our moral fabric, but do not imagine themselves as contributors to that decay.

The truth is, at a certain level, many Americans are as "good" perhaps as the Pharisee in Luke's famous story. While in Christian circles it has been customary to castigate Pharisees, let us remember they were often very good people. Most of us, including ministers, perhaps especially ministers, would love to have them in our churches.

Why? For one thing, they took their religion seriously. They never missed a Sabbath service at the synagogue. You would never find devout Pharisees consenting to organized sports on the Sabbath morning. Many Pharisees knew much of their Bible by memory and to top it off, most of them were tithers, which means they gave 10% of their income to the synagogue and temple. That's why Jesus once told his disciples that unless their righteousness exceeded that of the Pharisees, they would not enter the kingdom.

Yet, for all their goodness, some Pharisees had one fatal flaw. Their goodness and righteousness often blinded them to the subtleties of pride and arrogance. Their vigorous, external law-keeping often caused them to overlook the sins in the depths of their heart and soul. Sins like greed and avarice, lust and censoriousness, snobbishness and a moral unctuousness, which made them repulsive.

Since the Pharisee in Luke's story seems to display some of these undesirable qualities, he reminds us of some of our Puritan ancestors who, in their moral and religious earnestness, were quick to sniff out sin in others, but who forgot that the greatest sin of all was lovelessness.

Simon the Pharisee may have been a kind of collector of celebrities. It may be Jesus had earlier given a stunning sermon at the synagogue and that Simon wanted to catch this rising star or perhaps even trip him up as an imposter, so he invited Jesus to dinner. But he gave him no customary kiss of peace when he arrived at the door. He did not pour cold water over his hot, dusty feet as any courteous host would do in that culture. Nor did he anoint Jesus in friendship with scented olive oil.

Simon is in many ways like Menninger's "good" Americans. His own goodness prevents him from seeing the deeper flaws in his own character that excuse him from responsibility for the corruptions of society. Characteristic of many Pharisees, many Americans, content with their personal assessment of their goodness, condone and often support an entertainment industry that exploits our every passion, elevates and applauds violence, and trivializes our most precious human experiences like sex, marriage, and family.

Americans deplore the corruptions that abound in our political, economic, and judicial systems but piously evade responsibility for confronting them. We seem unwilling to confess our complicity with deception and our easy acquiescence to evil. If the truth be known, many of us, like Simon the Pharisee, have a secret fascination and lust for the prostitute at Jesus' feet.

In his famous parable, Jesus asks Simon which of the debtors would love the Master most. Simon is no theological or ethical moron, so he answers, "The one forgiven most will love the most." "Right," said Jesus.

Ironically and strangely, we first answer the challenge to forgive by acknowledging our need for forgiveness, and then accepting it. In answer to Dr. Menninger's question, "Whatever became of sin?" we will not say, "I confess, George did it," but will say, "I confess, I did it. I am guilty of sin." Then we will know whether we are Pharisee or prostitute and that he who is forgiven most loves most. Or to say it differently, he who is forgiven much can rise to the challenge to forgive much.

II.

If the challenge to forgive means accepting our need for forgiveness, it then means our determination to see the potential good in others — even in our enemies. In other words, the challenge to forgive is the challenge to love.

That reminds me of the little girl who told her friend, "I want to marry a doctor so I can be well for nothing." The other little girl said, "I want to marry a minister so I can be good for nothing." But forgiveness means we should be good for something.

Orphaned girls often have turned to prostitution as a livelihood. Runaway American girls are sometimes trapped into slavery. Prostitutes often tell of a childhood of physical and sexual abuse only later to be abused by pimps and boyfriends as well as customers.

Prostitutes often are further abused by the hypocrisies of society that outwardly condemns them but inwardly wants them. Police can be bribed by prostitutes or can be solicited by police themselves. Politicians and judges can be bribed by prostitutes because they may be their customers.

Leading businessmen and professional people and corporations sometimes support a high-class escort system behind the scenes so that prostitutes often scoff at the external rectitude declaimed by officially righteous American society. So there is a sense in which the revenge of the prostitutes in the movie *Unforgiven* is understood if not justified.

The prostitute in our biblical story was more fortunate because she had met Jesus and heard his sermons about God's all-inclusive grace and love. Perhaps she had heard his classic story of the prodigal son and saw herself as the prodigal daughter being embraced, kissed, and welcomed as a whole person by the loving heavenly Father.

Perhaps she saw, as did the prodigal son, that despite the goodness of the elder brother, the heavenly Father can see the potential goodness shining through the all-too-real badness of prodigals and prostitutes.

Dr. John Shea states it profoundly when he says, "forgiveness is not magnanimously forgetting faults but the uncovering of self-worth when it is crusted over with self-hatred." Shea adds, "The graciousness of God focuses exclusively on the fact that although nobody deserves it, everyone gets it." Even our enemies. Or to say it again in Shea's words, "forgiveness reclaims the essential worth of the person" (*The Challenge of Jesus*, pp. 121-122).

The profound truth of those words is perhaps no more poignantly expressed than in the recollection of President Reagan's experience with his would-be assassin. Lying wounded in the hospital, Reagan said he realized he really could not pray for himself unless he also prayed for his enemy, the assassin, that God would make him whole. Reagan later wrote a kind letter to the would-be assassin's parents. Reagan could forgive because he saw the potential good even in his would-be assassin.

In our biblical story, Jesus does not make excuses for the prostitute, nor does she make excuses for herself. All kinds of sociological and psychological reasons could have been given for her behavior. Instead, she acknowledges her sin, as does Jesus. Even more, he acknowledges and affirms her infinite worth as a child of God.

Forgiveness is not easy. Many of us have been wronged, deeply wronged. Forgiveness does not mean we condone the wrong any more than Jesus condoned prostitution. Evil and wrong must be confronted and exposed.

Understanding why someone has done a wrong does not excuse the wrong or neutralize judgment of the wrong.

Let us not wrongly think that our increased insight into the whys of human behavior should undercut our courage to call wrong, wrong, says theologian Paul Tillich.

Yet, God sent not his Son into the world to judge and condemn the world because of sin. Instead God sent his Son so that he might save the world. As God does not bear the grudge against us that he deserves to bear, so he asks us not to bear the grudge against those who probably deserve it. Instead, forgive, that is, give their life back to start all over again. "Vengeance is mine," says the Lord, "I will repay."

Our task is to forgive and to work with people trying to emphasize their good after the manner of President Reagan. We are to accept their positive potential, to focus on building a new future together, rather than righting with revenge the wrongs of the past. Yes, justice must be served, but even more, mercy must be exercised, especially by sinners like ourselves.

The prostitute washed Jesus' feet with her tears and dried them with her hair and repeatedly kissed and caressed his feet as he reclined at Simon's table. She had been grasped by God's higher power, accepted by his inclusive grace, and forgiven by his unconditional love.

She poured the expensive perfumed oil of her profession on him, repenting of her past. She was, in a sense, forgiving all the men who had used and abused her, all the women who had condemned her, and all the hypocrisies of religion and society who had shunned her while secretly admiring her profession.

She could forgive much because she had been forgiven much — accepted, restored, esteemed, and made whole. When we experience that kind of divine love and forgiveness, perhaps the challenge to forgive will not be so formidable. Or as Saint Paul put it: "Be tenderhearted. Forgive one another as God in Christ forgave you" (Ephesians 4:32). Amen.

Proper 7
Pentecost 5
Ordinary Time 12
Luke 8:26-39

Demons, Pigs, and the Economy

Then all the people of the surrounding country of the Garasenes asked him to depart from them; for they were seized with great fear; so he got into the boat and returned. — Luke 8:37

In polite society we have not wanted to talk much of demons and the demonic. In our liberal, educated culture, we believe that sin was due mostly to ignorance and that evil could be eradicated by education. In our psychologically enlightened times we have avoided the more ancient religious and mythological language of devils and evil. We have instead preferred words like repression, impulses, sublimation, drives, complexes, phobias, regression, neuroses, psychoses, manic-depressive, schizophrenic, and schizoid — to name a few.

If we have been suspicious of religious healers, exorcists, and spiritual counselors, we have been implicitly trustful of psychiatrists, psychologists, psychoanalysts, counselors, and therapy groups. If we have been doubtful of prayer, meditation, and conversion, we have been trustful of amphetamines, barbiturates, and tranquilizers, not to mention alcohol, cocaine, and marijuana. If in our time witch doctors have disappeared, strangely enough witches have reappeared by the thousands. Even exorcists are making a small comeback after considerable media exposure and hype.

Whether demons and the demonic are widely acknowledged in our time may be debated, but that they were common in Jesus' time we can have no doubt. In his time, when most illness was attributed to sin, it was but a short step to attribute all mental illness or epilepsy to demonic power actually residing in the person and controlling him or her. Thus to cure a person of seizures, dementia, schizophrenia, or melancholia, the healer had to have power not only to name the demon but the power to cast him out — to throw the demon out of the center of the person's self.

In the ancient world, demons were almost beyond number. They could inhabit almost any living thing and take control. More than that, demons, and especially the prince of the demons, the devil, were thought actually to have the world under their control.

Thus, not only could physical and mental illness be attributed to them; catastrophes, disasters, and evil events of all sorts could be attributed to their power. Therefore, if one was to gain control of human life and history, one had to contend with demons and devils and to wrestle with "the powers of darkness of this present world," as Paul put it.

It is no wonder that the early church was fascinated with this intriguing story of Jesus and the Gerasene demonic. Mark's version of the story is probably the original. Matthew names two demoniacs in place of one. Luke, the beloved physician, emphasizes the man's state of mind before and after the healing or exorcism. More than that, as the only non-Jewish writer of the New Testament, Luke likes to emphasize Jesus' interest in all people, including Gentiles. (This exorcism takes place in Gentile territory and the cured man is asked to bear witness to his healing among the Gentiles.)

The early church was fascinated with this powerful story and so are we. If we are to have healthy lives and a healthy economy, we need to deal with our demons.

I.

Let us consider the demoniac. We may understand him more than we realize.

The gospels tell us he lived in the carved out caves or tombs near the Sea of Galilee. Ostracized from society because of his initial mental illness, the demoniac's condition is exacerbated by society's total rejection. Wild in his efforts to resist rejection and exclusion, the authorities chain him down by his hands and feet.

In a surge of frightened, defiant, maniacal strength, he refuses to be entrapped by the ancient equivalent of a straitjacket. He bursts the bonds, ripping off his clothes as a rejection of all constriction and runs wildly among the rocks, shrieking and screaming obscenities at the unjust, uncaring, hypercritical world, while bruising and cutting himself in the process.

Thus it is with considerable courage that Jesus comes into the presence of this terrifying creature. If the ancient equivalent of a tourist bus might have come within viewing distance of the "local attraction," none, out of fear for their lives would have dared confront this maniac.

No one except Jesus. Jesus, the integrated man; Jesus, the man in whom the centering powers of the universe found a home; Jesus, in whom the healing powers of God were focused; Jesus, the prayerful man at peace with God and with himself. This calm, strong, and fearless Jesus approached the frantic, frenetic, disintegrated man with faith and assurance.

Rather than pouncing on Jesus and tearing him to shreds, this frenzied, distorted intelligence falls down before Jesus and cries out, "What have you to do with me, Jesus, Son of the most high God? I beseech you, do not torment me."

The flailing, frantic, disintegrated man sensed he was in the presence and power of someone whole and integrated; someone controlled more by faith than fear; someone more loving than defensive; someone more accepting than judgmental; yet someone who would not patronize him or trivialize his illness or belittle his lack of strength to cope with the power that had gained control of his very being. "Jesus, Son of God most high, what do you have to do with me?" The answer was, and is, everything.

II.

He has everything to do with societies torn apart by the demonic.

No doubt most of us would resist being called demoniacs and many of us would hesitate to allow that our society might be demonic. Nonetheless, the more sensitive and perceptive among us see swirling powers and forces in our midst that threaten to take control of us and destroy us. The forces of disintegration and fragmentation make it more difficult to hold ourselves together. Are there not times, when as one person told me, when we are ready to strip off our civilized clothes and run into the wilderness shrieking primal screams of utter despair?

If the demoniac was schizophrenic, ours is often a schizoid, divided life, says the late Rollo May, popular psychoanalyst and author. Like the demoniac, we feel more and more alone, more and more empty, more and more rejected, more and more forgotten, passed by, and neglected. More than that, our inward self seems diminished.

Consequently, as Dr. May observes, "when the inward life dries up, when feeling decreases and apathy increases, when one cannot affect or even genuinely *touch* another person, violence flares up as a daimonic necessity for contact, a mad drive forcing touch in the most direct way possible" (*Love and Will*, pp. 30-31).

Like the demoniac thrust out of society into the caves and rocks, we seem thrust out of our self-hood in an impersonal, institutionalized, systematized, bureaucratic society.

How many of us have raged at another company's computer only to install one in our own company against which our customers rage? If we think talking with a business or company is bad, try talking with the government or the Internal Revenue Service, where you are assumed guilty until proven innocent.

In a society where we feel oppressed or powerless, in a system where we feel inconsequential and exploited, in a culture that seems controlled by alien forces, we react like the demoniac in violence or distorted sexuality. In an effort to touch someone, in a craving to know and to be known, in an effort to be something more than a social security number on an IRS form, in our struggle to be more than middle- or upper-middle class serfs to a government despicably wasteful; in such an effort, is it any wonder we react in violence and distorted sexuality in a desperate effort to feel, be connected, count somehow, and make a difference?

Our schizoid world may not be far from that of the demoniac's. If artists and neurotics are predictive and prophetic as Dr. May suggests, Picasso's painting *Guernica*, with its fragmented bulls and torn villages of modern war, is predictive. The atrocities of our wars, the wasted lives, the utter, barbaric brutality, the waste, the disorder, the lack of discipline, the drug addiction, and mental derangement — the smoke and blood of real battle on our televisions during our cocktail hour — all this is a symbol of the disjointedness and disintegration of our own society — a society not unlike that of the demoniac.

So in the ancient despair we shriek, "Jesus, Son of the most high God, what do you have to do with us?" And he answers firmly and quietly, "What is your name?" We reply, "Legion," for like the ancient demoniac who may have gone berserk after witnessing the horrible atrocities of war, we too say "Legion," 6,000 demons like a legion of Roman soldiers exerting terrible power and influence over us and our society.

Then Jesus says, "Come out of him, come out of them." In the context of the church, in the surroundings of the worshiping community, amid a people committed to wholeness and balance, to saneness and integration, amidst a people singing and praying and centering on God in faith, hope, and love — in such a context, the powerful, peaceable voice of Jesus is heard, saying, "Come out of them, you negative, destructive demonic power. Come out of them, you oppressive ideas, you controlling compulsions and obsessions. Come out of them you powers of guilt, regret, and revenge. Come out of them you faulty self-images and harmful habits. Release them. Let them go. Be healed. Peace be with you."

Again Jesus comes, making his assault on demoniacs and demonic societies, making them whole and peaceful and integrated. Christ's gospel, says historian T.R. Glover, "took terror out of men's souls… and greatly purified and sweetened life. Whenever the church returns to him there is a resurrection," says Dr. Glover, "an evidence of new life. As the demoniac was made whole, so might we be" (*Jesus in the Experience of Men*, pp. 7, 13).

III.

If Jesus has power to heal demonic societies, he also has power to change economies.

When you think of it, there may have been some humor in this story. Consider this: Jesus, a practicing Jew, consorting among Gentiles who, of all things, were raising forbidden pigs for non-kosher pork. Even more ironic, it may have been some back-sliding Jews who were raising the forbidden pigs to sell at good profit to the neighboring Gentiles.

When looking for a place to put the 6,000 demons, Jesus honored the demons' request to go into 2,000 pigs (that's three demons per pig!). Now demon possessed, the pigs, in a demonic frenzy, rush off the cliff into the lake and drown. So much for the forbidden pigs and non-kosher pork. At least, thought the more faithful and Orthodox Jews, the pigs were put to good use!

The economic question here is, is a man worth 2,000 pigs? The former demoniac is now sitting calmly at Jesus' feet, clothed, sane, whole, peaceful, and ready to lead a productive life as Jesus' disciple to the Gentiles. Think of it, from demoniac to disciple. But the herdsmen, thinking of the lost pigs, ran into the city to tell the owners. They in turn came rushing out to the scene. In disbelief they saw the wild demoniac they had rejected and chained now sitting peaceably and calmly in his right mind. They were amazed.

Then another reality took hold of them — the reality of lost ham, bacon, and pork chops. I don't know how many of you trade in hogs and pork bellies, but I recently noticed hog futures were about $.90 per pound. So for a herd of hogs at an average of 150 pounds per hog, those 2,000 pigs were worth about $288,000 by today's prices! Is it worth 2,000 pigs or $288,000 to cure one demoniac? What if the pigs belonged to you or me?

Should we care more for dollars or for people? If our pigs had been lost, would we have focused more on them than on the man made whole? Would we, like the Gerasenes, ask Jesus to leave our city, country, and economy? Have we? One scholar quips sadly, "All down the ages the world has been refusing Jesus because it prefers the pigs" (Levertoff, quoted in *Matthew*, Tyndale New Testament Commentaries, R.V.G. Tasker, p. 94). It doesn't need to be pigs or healing. It can be both.

Bill Gates, America's richest man, dropped out of Harvard to start what is now Microsoft. He went back to Harvard in 2007 to give the commencement address and they awarded him his degree much to his attorney father's relief.

Concerned now about world poverty and disease, Bill Gates and his wife, Melinda, have set up a foundation with $33 billion to address health and education issues. Warren Buffet, America's second richest man, will contribute another $30 billion to the Gates Foundation to make it the world's largest charitable organization.

Bill Gates told his Harvard audience that at one time he had no real awareness of the appalling disparities of health and wealth that condemn millions to despair. When he got more involved in charitable work, he assumed the world would make it a priority to discover and deliver medicine to save the millions of dying children. But the world did not. In the words of our text, "saving the pigs," that is, saving the prevailing economy and mindset, was more important than saving children.

So Gates concludes that we "can make market forces work better for the poor if we can develop a more creative capitalism" (*Network World*, June 8, 2007). Yes, creative capitalism can make enormous strides toward making people whole and well. And when you think of it, the neighbors of the Gerasene pig farmers could each have contributed some pigs to build a new herd to compensate for the loss. A man is worth 2,000 pigs especially when it is our man.

When Jesus comes into an area, he not only casts out demons, he changes the economy because he changes people like Bill Gates, who was raised in the Congregational United Church of Christ, as was Warren Buffet. In all economies, rich or poor, Jesus calls for humane, compassionate, and creative ways to care for the mentally ill, the developmentally challenged, the homeless and helpless, the emotionally distressed, and the poverty stricken.

Yes, as in Jesus' time, we have our own demons and demonic problems. But Jesus has come to make us whole and to bring peace. May it be so with us. Amen.

Proper 8
Pentecost 6
Ordinary Time 13
Luke 9:51-62

Discipleship: Backward or Forward to God

Leave the dead to bury their own dead; but as for you, go and proclaim the kingdom of God. — Luke 9:60

It was Thomas Wolfe who made the saying famous: "You can't go home again." He said these words that have been repeated and quoted thousands of times since. It has some affinity with another saying, "You cannot step into the same river twice." Life, like a river, is an ever-flowing and ever-changing reality.

One philosopher altered the familiar saying to "you cannot step into the same river once," meaning that even as you step into the river it is flowing and changing and so are you. Life is flux and change and process. Perhaps it is because life is constant change and flux and process that we try to go home again to get our bearings, especially if we have a strong sense of place as do I.

I don't know about you, but I do try to "go home again." I like to revisit familiar places to recall wonderful happenings and to bask in sentiment and nostalgia. I like to return to my Wisconsin hometown to hike the hills and valleys, canoe the streams, and go boating on the Mississippi. I enjoy returning to other cities where I have lived, going to favorite restaurants, visiting favorite sites and bookstores, and looking up old friends. I even enjoy going back to Brooklyn where I once lived and ministered!

But times change and so do the places — the sacred places with sacred memories. Times change and so do the people. When we go back, we discover the people we once knew in a certain way have changed. Life is process for them too. And we have changed. Our hope of relocating precisely the feeling, mood, and happiness of a past event is a disappointed hope. Things do not come together quite as we had planned.

One time we were taking our children back to our home in Minneapolis in the suburb of Edina. We had moved away when they were relatively young and returned for a look some years later. Imagine our surprise when we discovered the stately, old elementary school our children attended had been completely torn down. There was an audible gasp from the backseat as they looked at an open playground where once had stood their solid, old school building sanctified with so many happy memories.

Our children couldn't go home again as far as school was concerned. The school was no more and even if the school had been there they wouldn't have fit in. Of course, they could have gone through the doors and revisited the gym and their old classrooms, but it wouldn't be the same, because they had grown and changed in so many ways.

Another problem in going home again is that the hometown folks, whoever they are and wherever they are, always remember you for who you were and not for who you have become. They remember you as a growing boy or gangling girl, from either the right side or the wrong side of the tracks. They filter you through their old spectacles of past realities rather than seeing you in the present for who in truth you are. It's hard to go home again.

Jesus discovered that it is hard to go home again when he returned to his hometown of Nazareth after he had moved away and become popular as a prophet. He spent about thirty years of his life in Nazareth, helping his father in the carpentry business and then taking over the business after his father's early death.

Now back in Nazareth, he is asked to speak in the synagogue, a high honor accorded to traveling teachers and preachers. Jesus read the famous messianic Servant Song from Isaiah 61, and then went on to imply that God had called him to be the Messiah, to fulfill that prophecy.

It took some time for it all to sink in, but it soon became too much for the hometown folk to swallow. Who does this Jesus think he is? We have known him from childhood, they said. His mother, brothers, and sisters live among us, and they are just common folk. Who does he think he is to claim that he is anything more than common folk?

We remember the houses he built, the furniture he made, and the barns he repaired. Now he claims to be the one fulfilling the messianic prophecy. Their anger grew to the point that they threw him out of the synagogue and tried to push him over a cliff to kill him. (These were the "dear hearts and gentle people" of his hometown.) The people who were looking forward to a Messiah for centuries were convinced he couldn't be from their hometown. It couldn't happen here and now.

So it was that even Jesus couldn't go home again – home to the people he loved and knew; home to the familiar streets, smells, and sights; home to the synagogue where he learned to read and write and began to memorize the sacred scriptures. There was a sense in which he had hoped to go back to God. Tragically and importantly, he learned that the way to God is usually forward, not backward.

I.

Perhaps that was what Jesus meant when he told the scribe that the foxes have holes and the birds have nests but the Son of Man has nowhere to lay his head.

I remember reading in detail the campaign arrangement of then presidential candidate Gerald Ford of Grand Rapids, Michigan. Every minute of every day and night was thoroughly scheduled by his handlers. He was brusquely hustled from one place to another to maintain a tight schedule. A news reporter called attention to occasional three minute gaps in the schedule. That, said a slightly annoyed handler, is a bathroom stop. Gerald Ford hardly had time for that while campaigning.

In his busy campaign for the kingdom of God, Jesus also experienced the pressure of a hectic schedule and the demands of the crowd. He had given up not only his family home in Nazareth, but he rarely got to his lakeside home in Capernaum. Such was the urgency of his mission and the message of the impending kingdom of God.

The scribe of our text, by contrast, had grown accustomed to the comfortable, quiet, circumscribed, and predictable life of the scholar. True to his title, he was a "scribbler," a writer whose task it was to copy sacred law by hand since there was no other way to copy it. As a consequence, he became an expert in the laws, knowing them almost by memory, and practiced more or less as a lawyer, giving learned interpretations of the law.

As was the case with most legal minds, his was backward-looking rather than forward-looking. When asked a question, he would look back to what was written in the law. More than that, he looked for precedents, past decisions, and illustrations from yesteryear. Reality for the scribe and lawyer tended to be located in the past. The present was to be defined by the past.

That is why Jesus' apparently abrupt statement was so much on target. Firmly convinced God was not to be found so much in the past as in the future, Jesus warned him of the risks of launching out into untried laws and cases and into uncharted seas. Was this scribe looking back to God or forward to God? Was he willing to leave the security of history and precedent to launch a new history? Was he venturesome enough to leave behind old definitions of sacred reality to discover and experience new sacred realities?

More than that, scholars and lawyers have "nesting instincts." They like to work within known boundaries of custom and precedent. They like to learn the established rules of the game and then play the game profitably and well. It is only the venturesome lawyer who will leave a safe practice and run for political office or become involved in social reform.

Better to lead the comfortable, successful bourgeois life than risk everything in a cause, no matter how noble, that may fail.

The scribe or lawyer "went home again," back to old sacred realities and securities. But Jesus, learning by harsh experience and divine inspiration, knew that you could not go home again. The way to God is forward, not backward.

II.

Another would-be disciple presented himself to Jesus and Jesus extended the invitation, "Follow me. Enlist in the cause. Become part of the campaign for the kingdom of God. We think the time is ripe for revolution and change. In fact we think the time is at hand. Come on board," said Jesus.

The would-be disciple obviously had been intrigued with Jesus, his message, and his followers, but when presented with the actual decision, he hesitated. "Let me first go and bury by father." But Jesus replied, "Leave the dead to bury their own dead; but as for you, go and proclaim the kingdom of God."

The dignified burial of one's parents was one of the most sacred obligations imposed upon a Jewish man of Jesus' time. The fifth commandment enjoined every son and daughter to honor their father and mother, and a decent burial and funeral was one of the ways in which honor was to be shown. Consequently, at first glance, Jesus' reply seems abrupt.

Let's take a second glance. Did the customs of the time call upon a young man to leave father and mother behind to serve in the army? Indeed they did. Patriotic loyalty then, as now, often superseded family loyalty. From time to time did young men leave home to pursue a successful career in places other than their hometown and native land? Indeed they did. The promise of success, fame, and fortune then, as now, led many a man to leave the burial of his father to others.

Something greater than career or patriotism is challenging us, said Jesus. We are announcing the kingdom of God. We are proclaiming a new political and religious order where God is king and righteousness and justice prevail. We want to draw people out of old ways of thinking and relating to new ways of thinking. Leave the spiritually and ideologically dead to bury the spiritually and physically dead. Follow me; join up to help create a new world.

The late Ernie Campbell, former Riverside Church preacher, liked to point out that many Christians prefer to believe in Jesus rather than follow him. They prefer to spiritualize and intellectualize the faith. They concern themselves more with right creeds, formulas, and doctrines than with right actions. They tend to see faith as a fossilized piece of the past rather than a living force of the present. They are not, as Blase Pascal observed, gambling on the supreme advantage of faith. They are at home in the old order and are unwilling to take risks for the new order.

They remain mildly content with their parents' definition of reality rather than shaping new realities. Unlike Jesus, who had the courage to leave the repressive atmosphere of Nazareth, this disciple went home again and stayed home, devoted to the old order until at last he was buried in it.

Alas, said Jesus, the way to God is not backward, but forward. God is interested in creating a new future. Go, proclaim the kingdom of God.

III.

The third backward-looking, would-be disciple wanted first to go say good-bye to those at home. Jesus gave his now-famous reply, saying, "No one who puts his hand to the plow and looks back is fit for the kingdom of God."

I doubt if there are many who have had the experience of plowing in the manner of a Palestinian farmer of Jesus' day. Hitched to an ox or a donkey, the farmer would guide his plow carefully, keeping his eye on a distant, fixed point so as to plow a straight furrow. The only way to do the job right was to look forward. Look ahead to how much you had to do and do well. Look ahead to the opportunity for new life and growth in freshly tilled fields rather than looking back to the past, to what has already been accomplished. If you look back, your furrows will be crooked and your future will be troubled.

Jesus was fearful this young man believed he could go home again and that once he got there he would be content to rest on his laurels and stay there. Like a friend of mine who was a high school basketball star and always going back to the memories of his past glory rather than creating a new future. Jesus was afraid this young man would be enticed by the memories of the past rather than be challenged by the promise of a new future.

Many of us have encountered people like that. "If only you had been there," they tell us. "Those were the days, the good old days, when God was in his heaven and all was right with the world." It doesn't take long for us to figure out that they are not really with us, they are not only remembering the past but living in the past. They've gone backward to

God, backward to the sacred moments, backward to the way it used to be but isn't now and never will be again.

Those of us in religion are prone to look backward to God — and with good reason. If philosophers look back to the Axial Period 600 years before Christ and the burst of insight and philosophy characteristic of that period, so do we look back to Moses, Isaiah, Jesus, and Paul as high points of the experience of God in human history.

Consequently, ministers tend to get buried in ancient books and dusty tomes. We poke around in archeological digs for evidence of a far-off divine event. We collect our relics, visit our museums, recall the past heroes of the faith, and sing and play music that is more a museum piece than a march or dance.

Sometimes we get the feeling that we spend most of our time and energy remembering other people's sacred moments and peak experiences. We talk about other people's encounters with God but do not take the risk of having some of our own. We tend to live out other people's past definitions of reality. We conform to their taste, succumb to their fears and biases, and constrict ourselves to their experiential boundaries. We've gone back to say good-bye to our family and stayed there within the confines of those old realities. Ministers are in danger of that.

It's a little like being born into a family who talks only of things that happened before you were born. Pretty soon, you get the idea that you do not belong, that you are really an outsider, that all the sacred and important events happened before you got here and cannot happen again. Too bad. You missed out. God came this way once and never will come again. We'll tell you the stories, but the memories and realities really are ours, not yours.

That's what the hometown folk told Jesus of Nazareth. His suggestion that the kingdom of God was breaking into history in a new way in their own time even through a hometown boy was just too much.

So they tried to kill him. He was disturbing the sacred memories. He was undermining the old definitions of reality. He was bringing into the present what they had locked into the past or safely postponed to the distant future. He was challenging them to new ways of seeing and relating. He was shocking them out of the comforts of sentiment and nostalgia in to the searing demands of a God who asks for justice and righteousness now, who requires a pilgrimage of faith and hope and love now with a Jesus who says with philosopher Alfred North Whitehead that "without adventure civilization is in decay," who affirms again with Whitehead that "Advance or Decadence are the only choices offered to humankind. The pure conservative is fighting against the essence of the universe" (*Adventures in Ideas*, p. 354).

Jesus had it right, once you set your hand to the plow, you can't look back. You can't go home again. The way to God is forward, not backward. Amen.

**Proper 9
Pentecost 7
Ordinary Time 14
Luke 10:1-11, 16-20**

How to Get the Job Done

And [Jesus] said to them, "The harvest is plentiful, but the laborers are few; pray therefore the Lord of the harvest to send out laborers into his harvest." — Luke 10:2

It's a startling fact but true — Jesus and politicians have a lot in common. This no doubt comes as a surprise to those who regard politics as a dirty business, or who think of politicians essentially as liars and who believe steadfastly that politics and religion don't mix. Nonetheless, Jesus and politicians have a lot in common.

When you think of it, politicians are elected by promising us something better. Many years ago President Reagan was elected and then re-elected by asking the public, "Are you better off now than four years ago?" The first time, the people answered "no," and elected Reagan for the promise of something better. Four years later they responded "yes" to the question and elected Reagan for another term in hope of an even better four years.

Jesus and politicians do have a lot in common. Not always, however. A little girl asked her mother whether all fairy tales began with "Once upon a time." "No," replied the mother. "Today most of them begin with, 'If I'm elected.' " Jesus made promises, but not like that.

Was Jesus, 2,000 years ago, promising something better? Indeed he was. He said he came to bring in the kingdom of God, the rule of God's righteousness in the world. For 900 years Jews had been hoping for a restoration of the glorious kingdom of David and Solomon. For 500 years they had been longing for an end to foreign tyranny and a return to prosperity and freedom. In Jesus' time, the longings and expectations were at an all-time high.

For Jews of that time, the hopes of a better life were often focused on a Messiah, a new King David who would come and restore their good fortune. Others spoke of a messianic age about to arrive, the coming of the kingdom of God, a time when God would reign supreme over his people — when freedom and prosperity and the good life would be enjoyed. It would also be a time when righteousness, justice, and peace would prevail.

Had there been people who claimed to be the promised Messiah? Indeed there had been, and the Romans, then occupying Judea and Palestine, promptly disposed of them. Now Jesus appears on the scene, announcing far and wide that the kingdom of God is at hand and that he is God's agent to bring in his kingdom, the new and better life.

Not only is Jesus like politicians in promising a new and better way, he is like them in his struggle to get the word out to all the people, to announce the kingdom coming, to raise expectations and to prepare them to receive Jesus' message. Without newspapers, radios, television, and the internet, how do you get the job done? You do it in person and you delegate emissaries — advance men — to prepare the way and to excite anticipation for Jesus' arrival and for his message of hope.

Politicians could learn from Jesus and so could businesses and churches. Wouldn't we all agree, he got the job done! After all, one fourth of today's world population, over one and a half billion plus people, claim to be Jesus' people and that doesn't even count the millions who have preceded us in the previous twenty centuries.

How do we get the job done in our time? Our text gives us clues. Here they are.

I.

The first thing we learn from Jesus is to delegate.

Delegation is more difficult than it sounds. Delegation is especially difficult for talented and extraordinary leaders, and even more difficult for leaders who seem to have a special calling from God.

That was the case with Moses some thirteen centuries before Christ. After successfully leading the Israelites out of slavery in Egypt toward freedom in the Promised Land, Moses had problems with a somewhat rebellious and cantankerous group.

So he complained to God, "I am not able to carry all this people alone, the burden is too heavy for me" (Numbers 11:14). In fact, Moses was so discouraged, he asked God to kill him unless he helped him.

God asked Moses to gather seventy men who he knew to be natural leaders and officers and to bring them to the tent of meeting, where God manifested his presence. God said, "I will come down and talk with you there; and I will take some of the spirit which is upon you and put it upon them; and they shall bear the burden of the people with you, that you may not bear it yourself alone" (Numbers 11:17). So God's Spirit did come upon the seventy and Moses had people to whom he could delegate responsibility and leadership.

Thirteen centuries later, Jesus uses the same number — seventy — to recruit men to help him spread the word about the new kingdom of God. If Moses and the seventy elders were developing the Old Israel, Jesus and the seventy were about to develop the New Israel.

In Jesus' case, the seventy signify something more. If the twelve apostles were originally sent to the lost sheep of the tribes of Israel, the seventy have a broader mission. They are to announce the coming kingdom not only to the Jews, but to Samaritans and Gentiles as well. In Jesus' day, it was popularly believed there were seventy nations in the world. Thus, Jesus' seventy disciples symbolized his universal mission to all the nations — Gentiles and Samaritans included. All the outsiders were now invited to be insiders.

Delegation is difficult for gifted, energetic people like Moses and Jesus because they fear no one can do the job quite as well as they. And they probably are right. Yet, without delegation even the most talented and energetic leaders will burn out or wear out or both.

Besides, delegation by gifted, talented, energetic people to other gifted, talented, spirited people has a multiplying effect. Many people are just waiting to be recognized and given a chance to use their abilities for a greater cause. Thus, the leader who delegates wisely can multiply his effect exponentially — much like planting an apple seed to yield an apple tree with apples and seeds uncountable.

When Tom Peters wrote his book *Thriving on Chaos*, he had something like this in mind: that is, allowing for freedom and creativity by loosening control and delegating. It is precisely what a lot of corporations are doing — decentralizing, delegating, and allowing more opportunity for creative energy.

It is what needs to happen in church boards and committees — delegation. When spirit-filled people like Moses' seventy elders are given challenges and responsibilities, marvelous results can take place for the kingdom of God.

Do you want to get the job done? Follow Jesus' example — delegate.

II.

A second way to get the job done is to discover — discover new opportunities.

One of the common mistakes of people, businesses, and politicians who fail is their inability or unwillingness to discover new opportunities. Nearly every marketing success story in the last two centuries has had to do with building the proverbial better mousetrap and telling people about it.

Think of it. For centuries people thought travel by horseback and horse-drawn buggy was the way to go until the automobile came along, welcomed at first by derision and skepticism. And if for some the automobile was not fast enough, for others the airplane was a defiance of God's laws. "If God had intended man to fly, he would have given him wings." Some can still remember people who made that statement.

Failure is often associated with the assumption that, as things have been, they always shall be. Failure often is the inability to accept the new realities. Think, for example, of the Howard Johnson chain of restaurants and motels. At one time a nationwide leader, they have fallen on bad times because they took their definitions of reality from the past rather than the future.

Families sometimes fail for those reasons. Think how often we pass on bad habits from one generation to the next because we somehow think they are normal. Tragically, children who were physically or sexually abused turn around and physically or sexually abuse their own children. Even perhaps more subtlety and tragically, we pass our spiritual and psychological abuse from generation to generation. In other words, rather than discovering new opportunities for new familial patterns and realities, we repeat the old.

Churches do the same thing. If churches succeeded twenty years ago with a certain style and manner and approach, they often wrongly assume they can continue that pattern forever. As a consequence, many mainline American churches are aging and dying. The Roman Catholic church is experiencing a drastic shortage of priests and nuns.

Jesus faced a similar problem. Many of his contemporaries assumed the kingdom of God consisted in the restoration of a small but prosperous and powerful Davidic kingdom. They presumed the promulgation of a Jewish exclusivism started by Ezra and Nehemiah to address a need of the past. They were defining the future by the past.

Jesus, as always, was the revolutionary. He appointed seventy disciples to go to all people — Samaritans and Gentiles included. His kingdom — God's kingdom — was to be inclusive, not exclusive; universal, not provincial. "The fields are white unto the harvest," he said to the seventy.

If they asked where, he replied to look beyond their own fields, beyond their own backyard, beyond their own past definitions of reality. And that is what he says to the church of today. The fields are white unto harvest. The people are there and I'm delegating you to discover the new opportunities that are there to bring them into the kingdom.

III.

Want to get the job done? Then dedicate yourself to the task.

You will note that after Jesus pointed out that the fields were white unto the harvest he said to his disciples that they should pray to the Lord of the harvest that he would send forth laborers. The harvest is plentiful, but the laborers are few. Pray, therefore for dedicated laborers.

Some years ago Russell Conwell wrote a best-selling book, *Acres of Diamonds*. He pointed out that the world is full of diamond-like opportunities for those with eyes to see. One reason people are not dedicated to mining the acres of diamonds is because they cannot see the opportunities.

Remember the stories of people in Pennsylvania who were irked at the oil oozing into their fresh water for their cattle — irked that is, until someone discovered what could be done with the oil. Then they were dedicated to harvesting enormous fortunes.

The world, we are told, is full of willing people — some people willing to work, and the rest willing to let them. But the workers are on the side of Jesus and God. "I work," said Jesus, "and my Father in heaven works." If God shuns idleness and laziness, how can we, his people, not be dedicated to his work?

Jesus promised that we would do even greater works than he was doing if we act in spirit-filled dedication. And just as God gave some of the divine Spirit to Moses' seventy elders, so Jesus breathed on his followers the divine Spirit to be empowered for divine work.

Most any successful person will tell you that persistence in a task is a major factor in success. Many tell us that success is 10% inspiration and 90% perspiration. It is to be remembered that God is not only the divine, creative mind of the universe. He is also the divine, creative energy of the universe. God not only thinks, he acts. He gets things done.

Jesus asked his disciples to pray for laborers to help reap the fields white unto harvest. We may well imagine that when these dedicated, praying people finished their prayers, it dawned on them that they should volunteer to be one of the laborers — one of those delegated to discover new opportunities for the success God is wishing to give them. Because God, more than anyone, wants his kingdom to grow, to succeed, and to become more universal and inclusive.

However, there is a word of warning to dedicated people, because dedicated people can sometimes be foolish and wasteful in their determination. You will notice that Jesus told the seventy that if people didn't receive them and their message, they should shake the dust off their feet as judgment against those people and move on to the next new opportunity.

As the old saying has it: "If the horse is dead, get off." If people don't respond to the gospel, move on to those who do. If people, after repeated invitations, refuse to return to church, move on to those open and receptive to the gospel. "If the horse is dead, get off."

Want to get the job done? Most of us do. Jesus, our Lord and master teacher, shows us how — delegate, discover, and dedicate yourself to the enormous tasks at hand. Jesus and politicians do have a lot in common, except that Jesus delivers on his promises. He promised, "I will build my church and the gates of hell will not prevail against it." And the promise came true — a church over a billion strong and growing — growing throughout the world.

The fields are indeed white unto the harvest. Pray that the Lord will send us many dedicated laborers to go out and bring in the harvest. Amen.

**Proper 10
Pentecost 8
Ordinary Time 15
Luke 10:25-37**

The Good Samaritan (Revised Edition)

"Which of these three, do you think, proved neighbor to the man who fell among the robbers?" He said, "The one who showed mercy on him." And Jesus said to him, "Go and do likewise."
— Luke 10:36-37

It was a dark, rainy summer night on a remote road. David was driving home to his lake cottage after a movie in the resort village. Going around a corner he thought he saw it. He slowed, wondering if he had seen correctly.

He stopped, backed up in the driving rain, then moved his car toward the edge of the road, shining his headlights toward the ditch at the corner. Sure enough. There it was. A car overturned with its tail lights still glimmering in the darkness. It was obvious the accident was recent. There still were skid marks visible in the mud at the side of the road.

The driver of the overturned car was partially conscious and pinned under the steering wheel. David could smell gas seeping around the hot motor. He wondered about fire and explosion. Some miles from help and without a cell phone, David decided to try to work the driver free. After a struggle in the rain and mud, he was soon speeding to the county seat hospital, the injured driver moaning and half-conscious across the backseat.

Several months later, David was surprised to receive notice that he was being sued by the driver he had rescued that dark, rainy summer night. The suit claimed that David had compounded the driver's injuries by pulling him out of the overturned car and by taking him to the hospital.

David's body shook with the shock of unbelief and then burned with a slow, silent rage. He cursed his luck that he should have come upon that car that night. He wondered then why he hadn't gone on to leave the driver there while he got more help. He remembered the gas dripping on the hot motor, the threat of fire and explosion, and the danger to his own life as well as the driver's. David wondered what kind of human being it was who could sue the man who saved his life. Instead of a hero's medal or thank-you letter, it was a lawsuit. When he calmed down, he called his lawyer.

David's is not an isolated case. Numerous Americans have been hauled into court for being Good Samaritans who, it was claimed, either aggravated or increased the extent of injury of the victim they saved. If doctors have had to defend themselves against the proliferation of malpractice suits, Good Samaritans have increasingly found themselves in court being sued for an act of mercy.

So, the question arises, what kind of society are we anyway when people sue their fellow citizens for attempting to save their lives? Is it too dangerous to be a good neighbor anymore? Is it advisable to be a Good Samaritan? Is the Good Samaritan really a model for Christians in today's society? Are the lawyer, the priest, and the Levite better models? Whom should we emulate?

I.

Consider the lawyer. It was his question that precipitated Jesus' story. After all, he was asking afresh, just who is my neighbor? Who am I obligated to help? If the second great commandment says love thy neighbor as thyself, who is to be considered my neighbor? David surely wondered about that as he drove to see his lawyer to prepare his defense.

The lawyer of Jesus' day would have been knowledgeable in religious and civil law because they were closely intertwined in his society. A good Jew was one who kept the law, all 613 commandments of the law. There were 365 negative commandments, one "thou shalt not" for every day of the year, and 248 positive commandments, or "thou shalts."

Undoubtedly the lawyer knew the legal ramifications of helping other people. He knew it was possible to get into trouble giving assistance to those in need. A friend in need may be a friend indeed, but he had also learned what a friend of mine believes and that is a friend in need is a friend to avoid! Wishing to avoid as many friends in need as possible, wishing to keep his life free of encumbrances and involvement, and desiring to justify himself, he asked Jesus, who is my neighbor?

Many Americans have the lawyer's frame of mind. Next to Israel, America is the most litigious country in the world. We are ready to sue most anyone at the drop of a hat. Frustrated, angry, and desperate about the complexities of modern life, we seek restitution in the courts! Add to that the cascade of government rules and regulations, at once the lawyer's spawning ground and livelihood, and it is no wonder we have more lawyers per capita, more per square city block, than any country save ancient Israel.

Someone quipped that in the Middle East they have billboards that read, "Love Thy Neighbor," followed immediately by six paragraphs of small print! With a little imagination we can envision Good Samaritan kits created by the legalists, which would contain "Waiver of Liability" forms the victim would have to sign before he could be helped.

Hooked on law, legalists always want to justify themselves as did this lawyer in Jesus' story. Convinced law is more real than love, they take a defensive stance behind the legal code, careful never to make themselves vulnerable and careful, therefore, never to risk love. Left to the legalists, the hapless victim on the Jericho Road would still be wounded and bleeding in the ditch.

Give us a society of legalists and soon our cities will be centers of terror and fear, for no one will come to our aid to help us when mugged. Give us a society of legalists and the libraries will be inundated with law books and legal codes, forcing out the great, creative literature.

Give us a country of legalists and soon the legal departments of corporations will be larger than research, development, and production. Give us a society of legalists and we will have churches straining at a gnat of religious rules and swallowing a camel of inhumanity to man.

Give us a society of legalists where every tenth citizen is a lawmaker, regulator, policeman, bureaucrat, or lawyer, and we soon will be tied down like Gulliver, able to break free only by raging revolution and the love of freedom and the freedom to love.

Jesus forever condemned the legalistic model for society. Consequently, lawyers and lawmakers of today who follow Jesus have the awesome responsibility to lead us to a more equitable society where we are free to love. Rather than just reap revenues off our increasingly cumbersome and onerous laws, lawyers and lawmakers have the responsibility to create laws that help the Good Samaritan rather than hinder him. We are obligated to create laws that expedite love rather than squelch it; laws that encourage neighborliness rather than discourage it.

Let lawyers and lawmakers take the lead in creating laws that aid the victim and his helpers rather than penalize them and help the criminal. If there is a great concern for criminal justice, let there be equal concern for justice for victims and Good Samaritans.

Who is my neighbor? asked the lawyer, seeking to justify himself. Jesus drew none of the ancient distinctions of humankind — Greek and barbarian, Roman citizen and foreigner, freeman and slave, Jew and Gentile. Rather, Jesus told him how to be neighborly wherever he was to whomever he could help in need. He told him to go beyond the withdrawn, defensive, legalistic model for life and to be a loving, caring person.

II.

In Jesus' classic story the religious types are not held up for admiration either. As representatives of the aristocratic, religious elite, the priest and Levite were not, in Jesus' view, good examples of what it means to love thy neighbor as thyself.

The priest and Levite were part of the official religious staff who served the great temple in Jerusalem. Required to serve several weeks out of the year, priests and Levites often lived in the towns and villages surrounding Jerusalem. As commuters from the suburb of Jericho, they frequently traveled the desolate road from Jerusalem to their ancient city. The road rose 3,400 feet in seventeen miles. Its rough terrain and large rocks made it a likely place for thieves and bandits. It has remained so even into the twenty-first century.

In all likelihood, the priest and Levite were on their way to the temple for their religious duty. Their religious law stated that if they touched blood or a corpse, they would be religiously unclean for seven days. No doubt that religious rule was uppermost in their minds when they saw the victim in the ditch. The priest passed by on the other side. He wouldn't even come near. The Levite, perhaps a temple musician or maintenance man, paused to look at the victim and then he too went on his way. Religious duty called them. Ceremony was more important than charity, performance of liturgy more pressing than the pain of the man in the ditch.

It was precisely this kind of narrow, restrictive, religious legalism that so angered Jesus. He was impatient with religious people who majored in minors and minored in majors — people who tithed their mint, anise, and cumin but neglected the weightier matters of love and justice.

Jesus was forever impatient with narrow religious minds who were so concerned about keeping Sabbath law that they could not see the miracle of a man made whole on the Sabbath. He was frustrated with people who practiced antiseptic fastidiousness and called it religion. He could never understand the religious mind that thought it all right to pull an ox out of a ditch on the Sabbath, but not all right to release a woman from her physical bondage on the Sabbath.

It was the strangely negative, withdrawing, fearful, legalistic religious person Jesus so much criticized. When he was castigated for associating with the hated tax collectors and prostitutes, he replied they who are well do not need the physician, but those who are ill, do need the physician.

Religion should help those in need and not withdraw from them. The Sabbath was made for man, not man for the Sabbath. Religion should help life, not hinder. Religious leaders should be interested in touching the wounded and bleeding to make them whole, rather than withdrawing from them and loathing them.

The sinner Jesus denounced most often was the religious legalist who did nothing to help his fellow man. Goodness is not a passive morality; it is not a "colorless" abstention from certain vices. Most of Jesus' teaching deals not with prohibitions, says B. Harvie Bronscomb, "but with positive commands" (*The Teaching of Jesus*, p. 168). Jesus praises those who do good and not those who do nothing and call it religion. He is ever on the side of those who reach out in helpfulness, rather than on the side of those who withdraw in self-righteousness and defensiveness.

Who is my neighbor? Not this man, said the fastidious religious leader concerned about his ceremonial purity. Thus a religion that divides people in need from those who can help is not an adequate model for our day.

III.

The model for love, the model for a loving society, the example for neighborliness Jesus chooses is, of all people, a Samaritan. Want to know what it means to love your neighbor as yourself? Look at this Samaritan.

While filling out an application for a factory job a man was puzzled by the blank after "person to notify in case of accident." Finally he wrote "anybody in sight." No doubt the victim felt that way. Notify anybody, even that Samaritan.

However, that was hard medicine to swallow for most of Jesus' contemporaries. The Samaritans were a mixed breed. Ever since the Assyrians had conquered Samaria in 722 BC, the residents had intermarried with non-Jewish peoples. Roughly equivalent to Asians marrying Westerners, or African Americans marrying whites, the Samaritan offspring were the mulattos of their day and looked down upon — especially by the Jewish purists.

Perhaps it was because he knew what it was to be excluded and despised that the Samaritan had such compassion on the victim in the ditch. Since he had often been ostracized, unnoticed, excluded, and unwanted, he had a special pity for the wounded traveler. A traveling salesman himself, the Samaritan knew the perils of travel.

How was this Samaritan neighborly? For one thing, he did not give the victim what he did not need. For example, one summer at a northern lake, I had driven my motorboat across the lake at night to take some friends back to their cottage. When I was ready to leave the marina, my boat wouldn't start. One of the boaters said he knew what the problem was.

He grabbed his tools and began to board my boat, ready to tear my engine apart in the dark of night. Smelling his breath and noting his tipsy condition, I gently persuaded him it might be better to wait until daylight. Any mother of a three year old who wants to help mommy bake a cake knows there are times when help is no help at all. The same was true of the little old lady helped across the busy New York City street by two Boy Scouts doing their good deed for the day. Once across the street she turned to them in consternation and said, "But I didn't want to cross the street!" The Good Samaritan gave the help that was needed.

Note further his help was immediate, personal, and direct. He did not leave the victim in the ditch and resolve to lobby for better police protection along the road or determine to urge the road commission to improve the road to discourage bandits. He did not hurry on to form a committee for the improvement of Jericho Road while the victim expired from exposure.

Instead, he gave the victim what he needed then. He poured a medicinal mixture of oil and wine on his wounds. After tenderly applying bandages, he gently placed the victim upon his donkey and brought him to an inn to a clean room for rest and regular care. Out of his own pocket, he paid the innkeeper the equivalent of two days' wages and promised more on his return if the expenses were more.

It was not required that the Samaritan love the victim the same way he might love his family. He was not required to have warm affection for the victim; rather, he was expected to demonstrate good will and to help him in his need. It was not required that he be a combination lawyer, chaplain, and orthopedic and plastic surgeon to help the victim. Rather, it was required he help the man in the best way possible with what he had.

Love is risky. It is not stupid. It is not foolish. But love is vulnerable. Love does take chances. The Good Samaritans of the world do lay themselves open to attack either in the streets or the courts of law.

We must not let the legalists, the defensive, fearful, narrow exclusivist people bind our society in fear or choke it with laws that reward the bad and penalize the good. Any such revised version of the Good Samaritan story will not do for the people of the new day.

Instead, Jesus calls us to love our neighbor by being neighborly wherever we are. The gospel is not a declaration of rights, but a declaration of responsibilities. As one sociologist has remarked, even a slight increase in good deeds on the part of each of us would change the world. Indeed it would. May God give us the strength and courage to continue to be Good Samaritans. Amen.

**Proper 11
Pentecost 9
Ordinary Time 16
Luke 10:38-42**

Mary and Martha: Nine to Five and Five to Nine

(A Dialogue Sermon)

Man: Good morning! It's a pleasure to be here in the pulpit. But you may have noticed that I have someone in the lectern vying for equal time.

Woman: Yes, indeed. This is a feminist age, you know — a time of equality between women and men, a time for women to catch up on centuries of lost time in subjugation and oppression.

Man: That may be, but do you intend to regain all the lost time this morning?

Woman: No, but at least I'd like to make some progress.

Man: I don't blame you. Sometimes women have been badly maligned in our Christian history. Listen to this quote from John Knox, of the early Calvinist tradition. He said: "To promote a woman to bear rule, superiority, or empire above any realm, nation or city is repugnant to nature, contumely to God, a thing most contrarious to his revealed will and approved ordinances." (Knox must be spinning in his grave at the thought of a woman running for president!) By the way, the title of his book was *First Blast of the Trumpet Against the Monstrous Regiment of Women*, 1558.

Woman: Yes, and Knox should be spinning in the grave until he gets his thinking straightened out! I much prefer the enlightened 1963 statement by Pope John XXIII (*Pacem In Terris*, Peace on Earth) where he said, "Since women are becoming ever more conscious of their human dignity, they will not tolerate being treated as mere material instruments, but demand rights befitting human persons both in domestic and public life."

Man: You're not converting, are you?

Woman: Hardly. Have you seen any female Roman Catholic priests yet?

Man: No, and with Pope Benedict, I don't expect to see any. I agree with Pope John XXIII, however, and even more with Daniel Defoe who said in 1697 that "Woman… is the glory of her maker." That is why I'm glad you consented to assist with this text regarding two very important women of the Bible.

Woman: We need to hear more about equality for women.

Man: And we have been. I'm reminded of a delightful movie we've both seen. Remember Dolly Parton, Lily Tomlin, and Jane Fonda starred in a women's liberation comedy titled *Nine to Five*. Lily Tomlin is the office manager in a large corporate office. Jane Fonda is the newly divorced newcomer trying to learn the political ropes and newfangled machines of the corporate office. Dolly Parton, successful in her first movie role, plays the boss's secretary.

Woman: Yes, and the boss is played by Dabney Coleman. He is portrayed as the stereotypical male-chauvinist pig who regards female employees as well-paid waitresses and bimbos whose only job is to make the boss look good.

Man: Except for Dolly Parton, the secretary who is not only supposed to make her married boss look good but also feel good by hopping into bed with him. If the Queen Mother advised Prince Charles upon meeting Dolly Parton to look her squarely in the eye, in this movie it is clear the boss's eyes regularly are elsewhere.

Woman: In this lighthearted comedy, Dolly, Lily, and Jane eventually lock up the boss in his own home. While he is there, they introduce reforms into the corporate office — politically correct reforms, like on-site day care, staggered work hours, job sharing, and gender-equal merit promotions. Eventually the boss gets the credit and is promoted to Brazil, with the women ascending in the New York corporate world.

In a delightful way, the movie pokes fun at the stereotypical roles of women. It shows how effective and progressive they can be in the nine-to-five work place as well as in the five-to-nine domestic scene. They can be thinkers and doers.

Man: We have no biblical equivalents of Dolly Parton, Lily Tomlin, and Jane Fonda. We do have our text that accents differing roles for women. It is the story of Martha and Mary entertaining Jesus with a dinner party in their home in Bethany, a suburb of Jerusalem. It is a story not about mothers and children, but about two single women without children.

Some scholars speculate that Martha was widowed and that the home belonged to her. Mary apparently had never married and there is no indication their brother, Lazarus, had ever married. There is no mention of children or parents. It is a story not of a typical, traditional family, but of three single people sharing the same household.

Woman: There is no hint about what any of them did for a livelihood. Consequently, what they did in the nine-to-five work week is unknown. Perhaps Martha's inheritance was sufficient. But we do have in our text a story that has to do with the after-work time of five to nine. Whether we are mothers, singles, or men, the story has some insight for our family living nine to five and five to nine.

Man: Marthas and Marys have long been contrasted in our churches. We have had the Marthas, the doers, and the Marys, the thinkers. We have contrasted the materialistic Marthas with the spiritual Marys. The two have symbolized two approaches to life, especially the life from five to nine.

I.

Woman: Let's first consider Martha and let her represent the working woman — practical, career-oriented, materialistic, and determined to get ahead.

As we have said, we do not know the source of Martha's livelihood. That she had a house in suburban Jerusalem, we know. That she entertained at dinner parties, we surmise from our texts. On this occasion she planned a several course dinner — we can gather from implications of the text. Whether she went to work, nine to five, we do not know. But we can assume she was working hard, shopping, and then preparing food in the kitchen. In this regard, she was a good role model for some of the traditional notions of womanhood.

Man: Martha also seemed to understand the importance of material things. We can imagine she kept her home well. We also can imagine she knew where to shop for the best foods for her sumptuous dinner parties for celebrity guests like Jesus. We can imagine she knew the importance of money, especially since her husband died. Widows were especially vulnerable once their husbands were gone. As a single woman, Martha may well have had an early appreciation of money and position.

Woman: Women of today can identify with Martha. Women have been working for a better stake in the economy for centuries. As members of agricultural economies, they have worked right alongside men plowing the fields, milking the cows, gathering the firewood, harvesting the crops, and selling the produce. Indeed, the economy of the past was often centered in the agrarian home, where nine to five and five to nine welded into an inseparable lifestyle.

The separation of home and workplace came largely with the Industrial Revolution. Men, women, and children worked in the sweat shops. But when men began to make enough money, children, and then women, stayed home. Consequently, "the notion of the middle-class home, in which the woman's role is primarily that of a support to her husband and children, is a relatively recent phenomenon," says Anita Shreve in her book *Remaking Motherhood* (p. 14).

Shreve goes on to point out that it wasn't until the mid-nineteenth century that a woman's exclusive job became that of caring for men and children in the home. However, 20% of American women did work outside the home at the turn of the twentieth century. Nevertheless, a woman was to be the wife, mother, and homemaker.

Man: More than that, she was expected to be the protector of values, culture, and refinement. In the Victorian equation, a rather sexist equation when you think of it, men were regarded as base, vulgar, materialistic, and more interested in sex.

The Victorian woman was thought to be above such materialistic realities and strove to uphold the higher values — values that tended, however, to degenerate into fastidiousness and prudery. Yes, Victorian men put a woman on a pedestal, but then expected her to dust it.

Women did go to work during World War I and by the end of World War II, six million women were in the workforce. In 1947, 30% of American women worked outside the home, but the ideal of women at home as wives and mothers persisted.

But by 1984, fifty million women were working full time, many of them mothers of children who were still at home. Today, of the mothers who have children under five, two thirds work outside the home. About 75% of two-parent families have both parents employed. And nearly one half of all families are headed by a single parent, most of whom are women. Consequently, 80-85% of our children grow up in the homes of working mothers.

Woman: Women are working and working hard. Women now surpass men in the professions. From 1972 to 1982, the number of women lawyers increased fivefold and is still increasing. Women are becoming engineers, mail carriers, physicians and surgeons, insurance agents, heavy-machine operators, and airline pilots. Many mainline seminaries have student bodies that are at least one-half female.

Anita Shreve says that "women now resemble male workers in the strength of their commitment to the workplace..." (p. 18). They have increasing social ties to the workplace and identify themselves more in terms of their career goals and monetary success than they do as mothers, wives, or family members.

Of course, many women are working out of necessity. They are single and have children to support. Others, married or single, have college tuitions to pay or payments to make on the house, the vacation house, the boat, the ski condo, the Mercedes, and the club memberships. With all those obligations, it's hard to make ends meet!

Man: Martha, Martha, if ever women agreed with you, it's today. Good home, good address, good food and entertainment, material success and financial well-being are important. And women know it as never before. Even Jesus knew it, because the money box held by Judas contained contributions from wealthy women, some of whom even traveled with Jesus. (Rather risqué for the time when you think about it.) Jesus was frequently entertained at other dinner parties that cost money to put on.

Martha, Martha, you know the score. It is money that makes the world go round. Everything revolves around money, sex, and power. So use them all to your advantage in this tough world, whether it's nine to five or five to nine.

II.

Woman: But now let Mary take the stage and let her represent the other side — the spiritual, the intellectual, the ethical side of things. What about Mary nine to five and five to nine?

I have long felt that the Marthas of the world must resent the ensuing dialogue that takes place between the sisters and Jesus. I mean the Marthas who have had the almost thankless task of cooking hundreds of church dinners, the Marthas who have taken thousands of casseroles to families in need, the Marthas who have baked ten million dozen chocolate chip cookies for one reception or another, the Marthas who are there when you need some envelopes stuffed, some rooms cleaned out, some nitty-gritty tasks done. Marthas who will do almost all the dirty work — except windows — for no one does windows these days!

Yes, and after the Marthas have done all that; after the beautiful Martha of our story shopped, cooked, prepared, and served so that all, including Jesus, might enjoy a lovely dinner, after all that, Jesus has the audacity to say, "Martha, Martha, you are troubled about many things. Come and sit with Mary, for she has chosen the better part."

At that time, I can imagine Martha was almost ready to bop Jesus on the head with his dinner plate. "Isn't that just like a man," she might have thought, not unlike those guests who tell their hosts, "Come now and chat or sit a while," hoping, of course, their hosts won't until they have finished serving the food and drink.

Man: Martha had had a hard day preparing all this food. Whether her sister Mary had helped in preparation, we are not told. One thing we know, she was not helping in serving. She was listening to Jesus speak to the group during the several courses of dinner. Martha approached Jesus about asking Mary to come help her with serving. Could he not see she was in need of help? And especially could not Mary see that? Of course she could, and she ignored Martha's glowering looks in her direction. That is why Martha appealed to Jesus.

Woman: Does every family have a Martha and Mary? We did. While most of the family might be involved in preparing or serving a dinner, one daughter would have her nose in a book, oblivious to the pressing demands of the home. It is annoying and irritating to be working so hard to provide for our material well-being and have someone sitting there reading, thinking, or, God forbid, praying.

"I mean Jesus, can't you make those people see what's really important? Can't you get them in gear, get them to realize how tough it is to succeed in today's world, get them to realize how much they depend on our material and financial success? Come on Jesus, tell these thinking, researching, reflecting, praying, spiritually minded Marys of the world to get with it and help us in the really important things of life."

Man: If we can calm down a little and listen a little, we can hear him say, "Martha, Martha, you are troubled and anxious about many things. One thing is needful and Mary has chosen the better dish."

Woman: The Martha in us fumes, "Better dish indeed — as it turns out, no dish at all. She hasn't carried a single dish from the kitchen."

Man: "Martha, Martha, you are indeed a wonderful hostess and cook and a delightful connoisseur of fine food and wine. But despite all that, Mary is a connoisseur of things even more important — things intellectual and spiritual, things of lasting and even revolutionary value, things that will reverberate throughout history long after this excellent dinner is digested and forgotten."

I would imagine Jesus might note with sociologist Lyle Schaller that the primary place for socialization now is not the home, but the workplace. I imagine he might point out how our homes are designed to eat and sleep and watch television, but not to converse and share and nurture. Some of the homes of the past looked as though people really lived together there, knew each other, shared a lifestyle and value system, rather than just nodding in the hall on the way to the next activity with iPods in their ears.

Woman: If we identify primarily with our work rather than with family or spiritual values, if we are primarily money, power, and success-oriented, what does that say about child rearing and the values we pass on to the next generation?

Harvard's well-known physician-professor T. Berry Brazelton says, "The old myth of raising a child by instinct has disintegrated as our culture has become less certain of its values." He goes on to say, "How can we raise children by the principle of 'do what feels right' if we don't know where we're headed?" He then adds, "With the breakdown of the extended family and the disintegration of our cultural values, today's parents are working in a vacuum. We have," says Dr. Brazelton, "lost the kind of instinct that is directed by a culture or an extended family, and unfortunately, there's nothing to replace it yet" (quoted in Shreve, *Remaking Motherhood*, p. 125).

Man: "Martha, Martha, you are fussing and fretting about many things. One thing is needful, the spiritual center of life, and Mary, for all her faults and failures at dinner parties and material success, has chosen the better course."

Woman: I'm reminded of Tom Wolfe's sarcastic description of Manhattan social climbers, women in this case, who work hard, dress to the nines, and starve themselves into a chic, skeletal thinness that makes an x-ray technician's work superfluous. Joey Adams says, show me a woman like that who exercises morning, noon, and night, who diets to look chic and thin, and I'll show you one hungry woman!

Man: Hungry indeed! But hungry for what? Hungry for yet another material acquisition? Hungry for yet another social event, to see and be seen in all the right places with the right people, or to be seen in the latest "in" restaurant? Hungry for more success at yet a higher level in the career? Or increasingly hungry for spiritual truths that last and satisfy the soul and family for eternity?

Jesus said Mary chose the better portion. For her the issue was not so much living to eat, as eating to live; not so much the daily bread, as the bread of life. For her it was not so much a question of how we look or dress or eat or vacation or exercise, but how we think and pray and worship and nurture and teach and share and relate and serve and yes, how we love. Do we really love anyone but ourselves?

Woman: However, the spiritual breakdown of our society surely isn't due only to working women. Most of the people involved in the Wall Street scandals, corporate scandals, and the government scandals have been men. The breakdown of the family surely cannot be blamed on the working mother. Many men long ago abandoned family, church, and school for the sake of their careers, identifying themselves primarily by their jobs.

Man: If moral integrity and spiritual depth are to return to our homes and families, men and women will have to take responsibility. We need to stop giving approval to cheating in school, lying to authority, abusing drugs and alcohol, and cheapening and making banal the sexual experience. If our children are to become something more than worker bees in a mindless drive toward more, parents need to give up worshiping at the shrine of the dollar. The Marys of the world call us to our spiritual and ethical foundations.

Woman: The Marthas of the world are important and crucial. They get the research into practical application. They get the architects' drawings into a real building. The newly conceived product gets from concept to production, then to sales by the Marthas of the world. Without them the world, the practical everyday world, would screech to a halt and the trains and planes would never be on time.

Man: Nevertheless, Jesus said, "Martha, Martha. You are anxious about many things. One thing is needful. Mary has chosen the better." And what did Mary do? She sat at the feet of Jesus and listened as he said the true reality, the eternal reality, comes by way of self-denial and worship of God. With prophetic intuition, she anointed his feet with costly oil, anointed the feet of him whom millions would follow, anointed the feet of him who would turn the heads of history. Mary chose the better part.

Woman: Martha, Martha.

Man: Mary, Mary.

Woman: Who are you?

Man: Who am I?

Amen.

Proper 12
Pentecost 10
Ordinary Time 17
Luke 11:1-13

Our Father Who Art in Heaven

(A Dialogue Sermon)

> *And he said to them, "When you pray, say: 'Father, hallowed be thy name. Thy kingdom come. Give us each day our daily bread; and forgive us our sins, for we ourselves forgive everyone who is indebted to us; and lead us not into temptation.'"*
> — Luke 11:2-4

Man: If two of the sacred idols of our nation are said to be motherhood and apple pie, no one has ever exalted fatherhood and hamburgers to the American pantheon — although hamburgers are getting close! Despite the complaints of the feminists about patriarchal systems, American matriarchy has fared quite well.

Woman: Well, I have to admit that fathers have not come off too well in recent American history. I remember the old program *Bringing Up Father*, where not only the mother but even the children knew more about reality than the father. I admit I remember the long-running cartoon strip *Dagwood and Blondie*. Blondie is forever superior to the bungling Bumstead as are his know-it-all children. Even the family dog, Daisy, outsmarts Dagwood, whose very name suggests his inferior status.

Man: Yes, it reminds me of the salesman who came to the door and said, "Are you the head of the household?" and the father answered, "I certainly am. My wife and children are out shopping!" I'm also reminded of what the Duke of Windsor once said, "The thing that impresses me most about America is the way parents obey their children."

Woman: Or what Erma Bombeck said about parents. She said, "You become about as exciting as your food blender. The kids come in, look you in the eye, and ask if anybody's home." Or I like the way Ogden Nash put it when he wrote: "Children aren't happy with nothing to ignore, and that's what parents were created for."

Man: Possibly, but patriarchal systems are not always what they seem. For example, historically, Japan has had a patriarchal culture where the father was indeed the supposed ruler of the house. A seminary professor of Old Testament and Hebrew, himself a native of Japan, said that was a fiction. Officially Japan was patriarchal but behind closed doors the Japanese wife and mother ruled the roost.

Woman: Yes, that might be true. However, we certainly have had a predominance of patriarchal images in religion. Feminists have rightly pointed out patriarchal systems where the male is dominant not only on earth but also in heaven. Men, it would seem, were not only in control of families and churches, but of the heavenly realms as well.

Man: I understand what you are saying. However, even in recent patriarchal times, women have often run the church behind the scenes. Think of the enormous influence and impact of the nuns in the Roman Catholic church. And consider our mainline Protestant seminaries of today. Over half the student body is female. Fewer and fewer men are going into the ministry. Some would claim the men have been "feminized" out of the church.

Nevertheless, in the church, feminized or not, we still pray to "our Father who art in heaven." We read a Bible where the overwhelmingly dominant image of God is male and Father.

So in keeping with the Lord's Prayer to the Father, let us explore some of the masculine attributes of God and their helpfulness to boys, men, and fathers. There are three to explore — adventure, time, and ethics.

I.

Man: Probably one of the most dominant motifs of the Bible is adventure.

Woman: Oh, I like that motif. In my mind adventure has to do with wandering, sojourning, exploring, discovering, leaving home and taking risks, leaving security for the potential rewards of insecurity, risking discomfort for a lofty promise or hope. It is true that often in the Bible the model man is the nomad, the pilgrim, the one who seeks a fairer country and follows the nobler life. However, it would be much better if on occasion men would stop and ask for directions.

Man: You know, real men don't ask for directions! You remember the old joke that the reason Moses and the Israelites wandered for forty years in the wilderness was because Moses refused to ask directions. However, in the Bible the prototypical wanderer, Abraham, got his directions from God. God appeared to him, urged him to leave his country, his homeland, and relatives to go to a new land, a promised land where God would bless him. Rather than remain in the womb of the past, Abraham is summoned to leave the matriarchal nest to follow his adventuring God into a foreign land of promise.

Woman: Of course it is fair to recall that later in Israelite history, Moses is summoned by God to be an adventurer. When God appears to Moses on Mount Sinai and Moses asks his name, God calls himself "I am that I am," or "I will cause to be what I will cause to be." He then adds that he is the same God who had appeared to Abraham, Isaac, and Jacob.

Among the peoples and religions of the time, Moses might well have expected God to say, "I am the God of this mountain. I live here, I dwell here." Instead this God is movable, not only in space, but time. He was present to Abraham in Ur of the Chaldees and now he is present to Moses hundreds of miles away in the Sinai Peninsula.

Man: Well said and since God himself is an adventurer, he expects his people to be the same. So Moses led his people in the Exodus and the wilderness wandering where Israel was molded into a unique people of God. By contrast, matriarchal religions and gods tend to keep people in the confines of the womb, in the nest, in the comforts of the home and the security of the city. They favor the known over the unknown.

In the biblical religions, where God is Father and masculine, God's people are called to adventure and sojourning. They are challenged to explore, to discover, and to launch out into the unknown to make it known.

Woman: True, but you forgot to mention the women. Abraham's Sarah went with him on the adventure. So did Moses' wife, Zipporah. Don't forget they also left the comforts and securities of the past for risky adventures into the new future.

Man: You are quite right. However, we can urge boys and men to pray to God as Father so they have a heavenly role model for adventure, discovery, explorations, risk-taking, and the promise of new worlds and new realities. They are encouraged to leave home in the best sense of the phrase, to love God as an adventuring Father even more than the security of earthly fathers and mothers. They are challenged to leave the womb, to fly from the nest, and to be shaped by the God who leads them from the securities of the past to the challenges of the future.

II.

Woman: I agree. Another attribute of God as Father has to do with how we conceive time.

I have noticed that matriarchal gods and religions tend to conceive of time as cyclical. In other words, time repeats itself in endless cycles much as do seasons of spring, summer, autumn, and winter.

It is to be noted that the biblical, patriarchal religion conceives of time as linear. Rather than going around in circles or cycles in endless repetition of the same patterns over and over again, biblical time moves along a line. It has a beginning and it has an end. Time is going somewhere.

Man: That's right. We Westerners often forget how embedded in our culture is this notion of linear time. We speak of BC and AD, before Christ's birth and after his birth, when the line of time was intersected with a divine event. This event was not a part of the eternal cycle, but was an "interruption," so to speak, a time-arresting, time-altering event to change the course and nature of time.

Woman: We further observe that in Judeo-Christian culture we speak of the coming end of time, the *eschaton*, when history as we know it will cease and be consummated in God's grand scheme of things. Think of the fascination with the *Left Behind* series by LaHaye and Jenkins. Consequently,

Christians are urged to redeem the time because what we do in temporal, linear time affects our destiny in eternal time.

So we can understand the challenging words of Jesus where he urges us to love God over mother and father, who tend to be identified with the cycles of time — birth, growth, and death; birth, growth, and death! He who loves father and mother, that is security, more than the kingdom is not worthy of the kingdom, said Jesus in his startling words. Young people who want to wait around to bury the older generation before they commit themselves to the progress of God's cause in linear time will be left behind, said Jesus.

Man: Challenging words indeed. I think you will admit that matriarchal goddesses of the fertility cults were identified with soil, seedtime, and harvest; soil, seedtime, and harvest in endless, repetitive cycles. So we quite naturally speak of mother earth, not father earth.

Biblical, patriarchal God calls people to break out of repetitive cycles to make progress in the fulfillment of time. What has been is not always what will be. There is something new under the sun, but only to those courageous enough to break the grip of past cycles and patterns to launch out into the new horizons of future time.

Woman: I see your point. Such a God is a good role model for boys and fathers. Not a bad role model for girls and mothers, either, I might say! If women have sometimes accused men of being boring, stuffy, and anchored in the past, this biblical God urges men to "get with it." As God tells us through Isaiah the prophet, "Behold, I am doing a new thing."

Man: Exactly, boys and men who think they always have to go "back to God" have it wrong. The biblical God is "out there." He is God of the future, beckoning us to leave the grip of the past for the liberation of the future.

III.

Man: A third attribute of the biblical Father God has to do with ethics, behavior, and distinguishing between right and wrong and acting accordingly.

Speaking of ethics, I am reminded of comedian Henny Youngman who spoke of his father. "My father was never home," says Youngman. "He was always away drinking booze. He saw a sign saying, 'Drink Canada Dry,' so he went up there."

Woman: Another comedian said, "Hollywood kids always have a problem giving gifts to their father. It's not so much a question of what to buy — it's who to give it to."

However, returning to this matter of ethics, we should note that matriarchal religions and goddesses tend to emphasize consolation, comfort, and accommodation to the cycles, customs, and traditions of a people. Feminine deities are perceived to be more earthly, compassionate, and approachable. Rather than challenge us to some new thing, they tend to encourage us to relax and accommodate ourselves to the "way things are" because that's the way they've always been and always will be.

Man: There is a lot to be said for preserving established values and traditions. However, on the other hand, the biblical, masculine God tends to challenge the status quo and to interrupt the repetitive cycles of the way things have been in the past. No matter how ingrained, the past is never quite good enough. God is always calling people to a new future, especially in ethics and behavior.

That is seen clearly in the Old Testament prophets and of course in Jesus. Prophets characteristically are lonely because they stand out against the crowd and against the "herd instinct" and "group think." "Everybody's doing it" is never a legitimate excuse for those prophets who march to the beat of a different drum. "It's always been done this way" is a slogan loathed by those challengers of official corruption, deceit, and oppression.

Woman: Yes, I can concede that emphasis. Matriarchal deities are tied up with soil, seasons, and cycles and are very much identified with the present time and space. The biblical patriarchal God does transcend soil, seasons, and cycles. He is above all particular, limited time and space. Therefore, one can understand why he imposes high moral and ethical standards on all times and peoples to help them grow up into the moral maturity he planned for them.

Man: Would you not agree then that such a God is a wonderful father figure for boys and men of today? They are challenged to "stand up like a man" when it comes to important issues and morality. They will refuse to go along with the crowd just because it is the "in" thing to do.

Woman: Yes, I often have admired Martin Luther in sixteenth century Germany, standing before the earthly authorities, his life hanging in the balance. Rather than deny his strong reformation principles, he said, "Here I stand. I can do no other. God help me."

Man: There was Martin Luther King Jr. who said, "I have a dream." It was a courageous dream on which he staked his life for a better day of equality for all Americans.

Woman: Our heavenly Father calls all fathers, men and boys, as well as girls and women and mothers, to be adventurers, to make a difference in time and to change the world for justice, integrity, peace, and love. Amen.

If You Like This Book...

Maurice Fetty has also written **The Devilish Dialogues** (978-0-7880-1939-5) (printed book $12.95, e-book $9.95), **The Feasts of the Kingdom** (978-0-7880-1941-8) (printed book $20.95, e-book $9.95), **What's a Mother/Father to Do?** (978-0-7880-1878-7) (printed book $20.95, e-book $9.95), **Money and the Kingdom of God** (978-0-7880-1903-6) (printed book $14.95, e-book $9.95).

For other resources authored or contributed to by Maurice Fetty, please visit www.csspub.com and type "Fetty" in the Search box option on the left hand side of the page.

Other Cycle C Pentecost (First Third) Lectionary Titles...

Two Kings and Three Prophets for Less than a Quarter
Robert Leslie Holmes
978-0-7880-1719-3
printed book $12.95 / e-book $9.95

A Hope that Does Not Disappoint
Billy Strayhorn
978-0-7880-1749-0
printed book $12.95 / e-book $9.95

contact CSS Publishing Company, Inc.
www.csspub.com   800-241-4056

How Long Will You Limp?
Carlyle Stewart III
978-0-7880-1050-7
printed book $13.95 / e-book $9.95

The Chain of Command
Alexander Wales
978-0-7880-1047-7
printed book $12.95 / e-book $9.95

contact CSS Publishing Company, Inc.
www.csspub.com   **800-241-4056**

Prices are subject to change without notice.